COLLEGE
MINISTRY
FROM SCRATCH

A Practical Guide to Start and
Sustain a Successful College Ministry

A Practica
Sustain a

A Pra
Susta

A
S

Sustain a Successful College Ministry

to Start and
ul College Ministry

chuck bomar

youth
specialties

ZONDERVAN.com/
AUTHORTRACKER
follow your favorite authors

ZONDERVAN

College Ministry from Scratch
Copyright © 2010 by Chuck Bomar

YS Youth Specialties is a trademark of YOUTHWORKS!, INCORPORATED and is registered with the United States Patent and Trademark Office.

Requests for information should be addressed to:

Zondervan, *Grand Rapids, Michigan* 49530

ISBN 978-0-310-67105-3

Cover design: Toolbox Studios
Interior design: SharpSeven Design

Printed in the United States of America

10 11 12 13 14 15 /DCI/ 23 22 21 20 19 18 17 16 15 14 13 12 11 10 9 8 7 6 5 4 3 2 1

This book is dedicated to my mother-in-law, Joanne Walter,
who is now with our Lord.

CONTENTS

ACKNOWLEDGMENTS

Francis Chan: Thanks for taking a chance on me and for being such a great friend.

Chris and Sharon Newman: Thanks for your faithfulness in our church and for being so dependable and such great friends. Plus, I just thought it would be cool to see your names in a book.

Barbara: Thanks for being such an amazing woman, wife, and mother. I couldn't imagine doing all of this without you by my side.

Karis and Hope: I love you girls so much.

Matt Metzger: Thanks for your faithfulness in college ministry and for offering your insights for this book.

Scott Mehl: Thanks for your input and feedback on this book. I wish we could spend more time together.

INTRODUCTION (A BRIEF ONE)

Thanks for picking up this book. It has a unique purpose and design that I'd like to tell you about before you start reading it.

There are two main areas of ministry focus to college-age people: Campus-based ministry and church-based ministry. This book focuses on church-based ministry. In fact the need for practical resources for church-based leaders is my biggest reason for writing this book. It's not that this book isn't useful to campus leaders—I think it can be. And my desire is that the two ministry types will always complement each other, rather than compete. But it's important to know that this book's focus is clearly on church-based ministry.

Those who are familiar with my previous book, *College Ministry 101: A Guide to Working With 18-25 Year Olds*, may wonder what this book adds to the discussion. The simple answer is that it tends to be more practical with the day-to-day ministry side of things. Understanding college-age stage issues and adopting a philosophy of ministry and leadership (as I addressed in *College Ministry 101*) are still vital to your ministry. But this book takes things one step further into a very practical realm. It's a step-by-step guide to starting a ministry from day one, setting priorities based on the long-term needs of college-age people, and focusing on those aspects of your ministry in a hands-on way.

I designed Section One of this book to be read from beginning to end—like any other book would be. If you skip a chapter, you'll miss the flow of thought. I strongly recommend that you read the entire first section before reading anything in the second. It's the foundation for the rest of the book, and the content in those later chapters assumes knowledge of the first six chapters.

Section Two is different. It's designed to allow you to jump in and out as you see fit. Although you may choose to read it straight through, each chapter in Section Two is separated by topic, enabling you to skip around depending on your needs or interests. For instance, after reading the first section, you might wish to start small groups in your ministry. So you could jump straight to chapter 11 to learn how to do that. Or if you have a mission trip coming up, you may want to go directly to chapter 14. Again, read the first six chapters in the book first, but then use the following chapters as a resource to meet your needs.

Finally, this book errs on the side of simplicity. And by *simple* I don't mean *shallow*. I just mean practical. I hope my thoughts, experiences, and insights will be a starting place and serve as an inspiration, pushing you toward better and deeper ones that assist you in your ministry. The field of college ministry is rapidly growing, and I hope this book positively adds to that growth.

Thanks for all you do with college-age people!

SECTION ONE

Laying The Foundation For College Ministry

CHAPTER 1

THE PERCEPTION OF SUCCESS

My journey in college ministry began in the summer of 1999. It was a Tuesday night at Hume Lake Christian Camp, and I was eating dinner in the staff lounge. In fact I ended up sitting at a table with Francis Chan. I was a member of the high school program staff for the summer, and he was speaking that week.

I'd been doing a Wednesday morning seminar for the students all summer long, and I'd asked a few camp speakers to critique me. These were people who'd served in ministry for some time, were really good communicators, and had gained my respect for their character. I wanted to get their input, advice, and correction.

Since I found myself sitting there with Francis, I asked him if he was going to attend the session the following morning. He said he thought so. I told him I'd be teaching and asked if he'd be willing to give me some feedback on my message. I also asked him to please be blunt and honest. He agreed and we set up a time to connect afterward.

The next day Francis sat in on the session, and we hung out that afternoon. He gave me some great feedback on the seminar; but more than that, we spent almost two hours talking about life, ministry, family, and where I was in my own life. He asked if I had any experience in college ministry. I didn't, and I thought that would be the end of the conversation. (I was wrong.) His church didn't have a ministry for college-age people, so we talked about that for a while. Long story short, I visited his church a week and a half later and was hired part time to start "something for college students" at Cornerstone Community Church in Simi Valley, California.

My first day in the office was September 7, 1999. I remember it was a Tuesday because it was right after Labor Day weekend. I'd moved into town the day before, sort of settled into my room, and showed up at the church at 9 a.m. for my meeting with Francis. We shared some small talk, laughed a little, and then began talking about the college ministry. Well, sort of. He didn't really have any thoughts for me. This was great in that I had a lot of freedom, but I also had no direction or experience to go on. I had to figure out what I needed to do (or not do), where I should focus my energy, and where I was supposed to start.

Francis handed me the "database" of people who were interested in the ministry. It was a blue sticky note with six names and four phone numbers written on it. Some database, huh? This of course was better than nothing at all, but it certainly wasn't much. So I called the four people with phone numbers listed, met with each of them, and planned to host a barbeque at my house. I announced the barbeque one weekend during the church services, and I was excited to see what would happen. A barbeque wasn't much, but at least it was *something*.

Nine people showed up, including the youth pastor and me. We had a great time hanging out and getting to know each other, and it was at this point that I announced the next step for our ministry: A weekly Bible study.

I reserved a room at the church for our gatherings. I didn't want too big of a room, so I scheduled one of the smallest rooms available. It was a classroom with stale white paint on the walls, no sound system, and bright fluorescent lights. I did my best to make the room feel cozy, but nothing could really be done. We just left it basic. Bare bones. Everything we did was so minimal that we didn't even sing worship songs during our gathering times. We didn't have anyone who could lead. But eventually someone would lead the singing on occasion, and we used an overhead projector with transparencies to put up the song lyrics on the white wall. We gathered, I taught about some basic Christian beliefs, and we just got to know one another. Simple, but fun.

BEYOND EXPECTATIONS

I quickly found out that atmosphere and other forms of aesthetics didn't matter as much as I'd thought. Within six weeks about 50 people were coming. I didn't know *where* they were all coming from, but I wasn't complaining. Simi Valley is anything but a college town. There was just one community college in the next city over from ours. And there were two bowling alleys and a movie theater—that was about the extent of the "life" of our town. Later they added a mall, which was great, but that didn't come along until 2005.

Regardless of the lack of city life, we soon had to move our gathering to a different room because we no longer fit in that first classroom. And then we had to change rooms yet again. People just kept coming. So I eventually formed all of the typical things you'd expect in a ministry: A leadership team, a band, greeters, and so on.

In the summer of 2000, about eight months after we started, we had roughly 150 people coming every week. There was a great buzz in our ministry. I was teaching through different topics and books of the Bible; we'd started small groups; we offered a winter retreat, a summer camp—you know the drill. At this point I even hired a couple of interns to work about 15 to 20 hours a week. Our worship leader was one of them, and I also hired a female to work with the girls.

Everything continued growing numerically. People were coming to faith, and others really stepped up in various leadership roles. I started being very intentional about making connections on the community college campus, even taking a few classes to help me get more involved with the students there. And we had church members praying every Wednesday morning at 6 a.m. for the ministry, the people, and the city. There were all kinds of good things happening.

The next thing I knew, there were more than 250 people piling into the multipurpose room every Sunday night—which was a very tight fit. We'd originally set up round tables in the room because they helped fill the space. But we ended up taking all of those out to make more room for people. Every week it seemed like more and more young adults were coming. They'd hang out afterward until the early morning hours, go out to restaurants in droves, and all of our spots for the retreats filled up. We even had to take applications for mission trips and were turning most people away. It was crazy, but the ministry was everything I'd hoped it would be.

Then in the fall of 2001, we moved our group into the main sanctuary. This room was more than three times the size of the multipurpose room, so we again used round tables to fill the space. And we continued like this week after week as more and more people came. I was meeting with college-age people all the time, and I even hired more people. We actually had five interns in our ministry at one point. And by the fall of 2003 (four years after we'd started), we had a sanctuary filled with 900+ college-age people every week. They came from within about a 60-minute driving radius. People from all over somehow heard about our ministry and engaged in what we were doing.

GOOD VERSUS BEST

Now there's a reason I named this chapter "The Perception of Success." Many ministry leaders would love to have a story like this when they're just starting out. And this is what I initially wanted, too. But it's important to recognize that numerical growth is often a perception of success—not necessarily proof of it. We get that messed up way too often. I know I confused the two, and it showed in the fact that I missed some of the most crucial elements to having a sustainable and effective college ministry. I started one, but I wasn't set up to sustain it.

I thought it was cool when I received calls from other leaders asking about our ministry, or when they brought a team of people to observe us because they wanted to start something in their own churches. But when I look back now, we weren't nearly as effective in ministering to college-age people as was perceived. Sure, good things happened: People came to saving faith, and I talked about college-age issues that needed to be addressed. So, yes, God used it. But I didn't understand what college-age people really needed—or wanted—from me, our ministry, or our church.

I had some gifts of teaching and leadership, and we put together the right programmatic things for our context. But there was a point where I really started to question what we were doing. I looked at all of these people and wondered what our ministry was *ultimately* accomplishing—and I didn't have an answer. Sure, I could rationalize all kinds of things, but deep down I felt unsettled. And because of that, I began learning so much more about what it meant to effectively minister to college-age people.

One of the things I discovered was that our ministry wasn't sustainable. I did little more than create a parachurch organization that happened to meet on a church campus. I used to hear people talk about how great it was to see "this many college-age people connected to our church." But in actuality most weren't connected to our church at all. They were connected to our ministry. The perceived success that we experienced blinded me from seeing the need and desire for deeper connection.

If we stopped our weekly service, I wondered, *where would all of these people go? Where would they connect?* Unfortunately I realized that for most of them, the answer was nowhere. This is when my expectations, my definition of success, the role I saw our ministry having, my job description, what we did and didn't do—basically

> Numerical growth is often a perception of success—not necessarily proof of it.

everything changed. Everything. I discovered that effective ministry to college-age people was much bigger than having a large weekly gathering and doing college-age events.

FOCUSING ON WHAT'S REALLY NEEDED

If you buy into the false measure of success in numbers, you'll inevitably miss what college-age people need and perhaps want. They want more than a ministry to go to. They want to be connected to your church as a whole. And the earlier you realize this and put energy into building a foundation of connection, the more effective your ministry will be in the long run.

Let me be clear: I'm not suggesting that having a large gathering time for college-age people is bad. Nor am I suggesting that you shouldn't have a gathering point into which you invest a certain amount of time. What I *am* saying, however, is that college ministry doesn't *require* you to be a great teacher or to have a phenomenal band. It doesn't mean you're ineffective if the number of people involved doesn't grow by leaps and bounds. In fact starting from scratch doesn't even require another budget line, another program to staff, or interns to help run it. It just requires you to focus on a few things, do them well, and continue keeping the ministry simple.

If I were to start all over again today, I'd start differently. And this is why I want to take the next three chapters to describe to you that new beginning—what I'd concentrate on if I were to do it all again.

To do this, I'll answer the following questions:

- What's really needed?

- If success isn't measured by numerical attendance or involvement, how should you define success for your ministry?

- What are some ways you can measure that?

- What expectations should you put on yourself?

- Where should you start?

- How do you get people on board with what you're doing?

- What's the one thing you need to focus on?

After reading the next few chapters, I believe you'll realize—if you don't already have a hunch—that ministry to college-age people is very simple. Not a lot is needed, but I want to discuss those few things that are vital...

CHAPTER 2

CREATING AND MEASURING A SUSTAINABLE MINISTRY

....

The timing of my writing this chapter is a little ironic. Earlier today I met with a pastor and some staff members from a church that desires to do college ministry differently. People might wonder why they'd want to change anything because they currently have more than 1,500 people coming to their college-age gathering every week. Very few ministries have grown as quickly or have had as great an impact on an area as this one has. But talking with the leadership over the last six months or so, I've learned that—like others around the country—they've asked some of the same questions I shared in the last chapter: *What is this ultimately accomplishing? Are these people really connected to our church or any church as a whole? What's the purpose of our ministry, where is it heading, and how can we make sure the college-age people under our care are getting what they truly need?*

At the beginning of our meeting, the pastor said he wanted to download off my experience and hear about the processes I went through, what we did, and why. As a staff they've been thinking through practical steps they can take to be even more effective in their ministry, and I was honored to play a role in that thought process. It was a great two-hour conversation—over a nonfat, sugar-free vanilla latte (one of my favorites).

The leadership at this church has come to some healthy conclusions and serves as a great example to all who work with college-age people. The biggest change they're making might surprise you: They're ending their weekly gathering. Yep, they're not doing it anymore. It's important to point out that they aren't ending their ministry to college-age people. Quite the opposite, actually. They're going to take it to another level! I realize that ending something like this seems backward in a lot of ways because it seems so good. But, as I encouraged them during our discussion today, there is a big difference between what's *good* and what's *best*.[1]

---

1. I discuss this idea in more depth in *College Ministry 101* by listing seven concerns I have with creating a separate church service structure like this (pp. 27-30).

These leaders have discovered a need for something more. They happen to believe that making this change will be *best* for their ministry. I did something very similar at Cornerstone, but my situation was a little different. My priorities were focused on providing a great *experience* for the people coming to our service, versus really understanding and addressing the needs in their everyday lives. I'm not saying we weren't doing *anything*; it just wasn't our priority. This sent our ministry on a trajectory that might have been deemed good, but it wasn't best. If you're currently in the beginnings of your ministry, I hope you can avoid this same path. But if you're already headed down that road, then be encouraged that change can happen.

Back to the leaders I met with today: In order to take their ministry to the next level, they've redefined the role of the leader. His or her role will be to focus on meeting the needs (and desires) of college-age people through relationships instead of a large ministry gathering. They want to make sure college-age people are connected to the life of the church as a whole,

> Although there is a perception that college-age people are connected to their church, many are only connected to the weekly gathering. And this, ultimately, isn't best.

and this new leader will lead that charge. This is exactly what's *needed* in college ministry. They realized that although there is a perception that these college-age people are connected to their church, many are only connected to the weekly gathering. And this, ultimately, isn't best.

So you're probably wondering what exactly I'm saying is needed in ministry. And we're going to *begin* the journey of explaining those things in the next section. But first I'd like to issue a plea: If you're just starting your ministry, please understand that although putting together a gathering point for college-age people is a part of your ministry, it's clearly *not* the whole focus. I would have avoided so many problems and been much more effective if I'd realized this from the start.

If you're in a small church, be encouraged because you don't need a lot of the things that larger churches have in order to be truly effective with college-age people. In fact, from my experience and in talking with pastors like I did today, I'd say that in some ways it's easier for you to do what *really* needs to be done. And I mean that!

And if you're working in a larger church, I'd strongly encourage you to look beyond providing a weekly experience and into whether or not the long-term needs of the people you're seeking to reach are being met. Hopefully the next sections of this chapter will help you in that reevaluation.

SEEING THE NEED AND DEFINING THE ROLE

For many years now churches have struggled (some more than others) to overcome a generational chasm. Far too many churches have children up through high school students involved at some level, but then their structure jumps to investing in married couples and parents (or grandparents). Consequently college-age people and singles have a difficult time finding a place within the body of Christ. And although college-age people might enjoy having a ministry specifically designed for them, there is a much greater desire to be a part of our churches as a whole. This deeper connection is what's often missed.

It's for this reason that I suggest that a ministry to college-age people needs to focus on being a bridge for helping people find relational connection to the life of our churches. The role of college ministry is to move people from relational connections in student life to having relational connections in the adult life of our churches. College-age people are truly in between these two areas, and I believe the college ministry should help bridge the gap for them. No other ministry will do this. So if college ministries don't focus on filling this need, which has historically been the case, the generational gap in churches will only continue to grow. (See Figure 1.1 below.)

Role of a College-Age Ministry

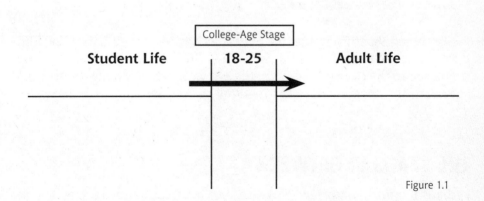

Figure 1.1

Please take careful notice of what I did *not* say. I'm not suggesting that our role is to move people from youth group to a church service. This might be a byproduct of the relational connections that are made, but it's not the focus. The focus is assimilation from certain relationships to others.

We all know that the time in a person's life between graduating from high school and becoming an independent adult is filled with all sorts of transitions. People move out of their parents' home and then back again. They go to school, change majors, drop out, transfer schools, graduate, or don't graduate. They take a job, get promoted, change jobs, get fired, and move to other areas. They date someone with hopes for marriage, break up, begin new relationships, struggle with others, develop friendships, and hurt some people in the process.

My question is *Who walks with these young adults through all of the changes, challenges, and confusion?* I think it's the role of the church. And, more specifically, it's the role of the college-ministry leader to make sure these people are being brought along in the context of relationships and in everyday life. This task requires more than a weekly gathering.

My issue was not having this role clearly defined in my own mind when I started. No resource pointed me in this direction, but I still I wish I'd thought it through. I ended up creating a ministry on an island of its own where college-age people were involved in our ministry but not connected to the church as a whole. They merely came to a gathering point once a week. Some were involved in another aspect of our ministry, but far too many of them went through all of their transitions and changes without a loving mentor voice speaking into their lives. We were able to change this dynamic over time, but this is the fundamental issue I'd love for you to avoid from the start.

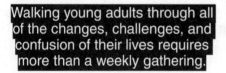

Walking young adults through all of the changes, challenges, and confusion of their lives requires more than a weekly gathering.

I've observed that the college-age people who have someone speaking into their lives in the midst of these changes and transitions are the ones who stay connected to the church. And when they stay connected during the college-age years, the generational gap is naturally closed through relationships.

THE YEARS IN BETWEEN

Perhaps the most important discovery I've made is that to be effective at making these connections, we must first understand the world in which college-age people live. Being aware of their world has everything to do with who they are and, therefore, what they need from our churches. By paying attention to the cultural shifts that shape them, we can see that now, more than ever, college-age people need faith communities to help them navigate the path toward adulthood. And the biggest shift we need to pay attention to is the increasing need for higher education.

The pressure to go to college has never been greater than it is today. In a tight job market, there's no question that a college degree is now a necessity. Where high school graduation was once the rite of passage into adulthood, it's now just a move from one kind of education to another. It's hard to feel like an adult when school is still the center of your day-to-day life—or your closest peers' lives. You're not a kid anymore, but you're not thinking as an independent adult either. College-age people have a foot in both camps but no solid grounding in either one. They're truly in between.

The increasing need for a college education often results in four more years of putting off adult decisions and thinking about life. These circumstances leave today's college-age people in the same position high school students were in a generation or two ago—still preparing for adulthood. This means they're heading toward thinking like an independent adult, but they aren't quite there yet. And it's also important to realize that this path toward feeling like an adult is taking longer and longer to walk. We see this in areas such as prolonged financial dependence on parents. But perhaps more objectively, it's seen in the constant rise of the average age of first marriages. Fifty years ago it was common to get married in your late teens or early twenties, at the latest. Today the focus of getting a college education before marriage has caused the average age to rise into the upper twenties for both men and women. This is one marker that shows the path to adulthood is getting longer.

My point is that the years after high school are no longer a time of independent adult life but a stage of life that requires the voices of caring and nurturing older adults. And although we know this in theory, we often don't embrace it in our ministries. Churches can provide much-needed stability for college-age people. College-age ministry fills a need in the lives of young people by walking them through this maturing process with love, spiritual guidance and care, understanding, and patience. What this ministry looks like will vary from one church to another, but the role of helping people navigate this space between adolescence and adulthood is universal.

> They're not kids anymore, but they're not thinking as independent adults either. College-age people have a foot in both camps but no solid grounding in either one.

Because these issues and cultural shifts aren't fully understood, college ministries tend to focus on getting people to show up versus helping individuals move toward the adult life in our churches. Helping people transition from having all of their relationships with other high school students to living life with other adults takes intentionality on our part.

MEASURING EFFECTIVENESS

If the main role of the ministry is bridging the gap by walking people toward adulthood, how do we know we're being effective? The number of people who show up to something isn't necessarily invalid, but we need something deeper than a head count. And it's far better to figure out what we want to see before we begin figuring out what we're going to do. Ultimately we want to see people move toward Christlikeness with the end result being their living out the call of faith in every aspect of their lives. We can measure our success in helping college-age people move in this direction by looking intentionally at how well we are—

1. Helping individuals process their age-stage issues

2. Cultivating quality relationships between college-age people and older, maturing believers

I'll briefly discuss these two markers here, and then I'll continue to come back to them throughout the rest of the book. Hopefully I'll show you how everything we do can, in fact, revolve around these two aspects of college ministry.

Helping Individuals Process Their Age-Stage Issues

Our ultimate goal in ministry ought to be guiding people toward the maturity and stature of Christ (Ephesians 4:13; Colossians 1:28). This requires us to meet people where they are, address the specific issues they're dealing with, and guide them toward biblically mature conclusions in each area.

As leaders of a college ministry, we play a small part in a lifelong process of discipleship. I've personally observed five overarching pursuits of college-age people that need to be guided:

1. Identity

2. Intimacy

3. Meaning

4. Pleasure

5. Truth

I will address these pursuits further in chapter 5.[2] But here I want to focus on the main issue: *Identity*. College-age people are thinking through who they are, who they aren't, who they desire to be, and how they fit into the world. And all of the other pursuits of intimate relationships (not just dating), meaning, pleasure, and truth help them answer these questions of identity. This is a long and complex process with many questions that need to be answered, but it's our job to help guide it. And if we're unable to be a part of this process of identity formation, then I believe we're failing in ministry.

I ask myself two basic questions in order to evaluate whether or not we're being effective in these areas: (1) *Do our leaders have a general understanding of these issues?* and (2) *Are these issues constantly being addressed somehow in everything we do?* If either of these questions is answered negatively, then steps must be taken to change that.

Put simply, one of the ways I measure the success of our ministry is whether or not we're focused on helping college-age people through each of these areas.

Cultivating Quality Relationships with Other Believers

While offering a weekly gathering point or small groups of college-age people might be a part of helping people sift through these areas, there's also a need to take this a step further. In my experience the most effective way of making sure we're addressing these age-stage issues, as well as forming deeper connections to the church as a whole, is by helping form natural, mentor-like relationships between college-age students and older, spiritually mature adults. These become people who, through a relationship, use their own *God-*

> Natural mentor-like relationships are one of the best ways to ensure college-age people are processing their age-stage issues and forming deeper connections with the church as a whole.

---

2. I devoted six chapters to a deeper understanding of these issues in *College Ministry 101* (chapters 2-7), as well as providing some training videos on each of these issues at www.CollegeLeader.org.

given experiences to help a college-age person navigate the maturity process.

When I understood this aspect and role of a college ministry, I completely changed how I measured success. It's so easy to fall into the habit of measuring quantity over quality. We can obviously measure the amount of mentorships that are happening. But just because people are assigned a mentor—or mentee—that doesn't mean it's effective. Although the number of people involved might suggest that we're doing something right, it doesn't help us see those areas that need attention. And this is why we need to have additional measurements, namely the *quality* of the relationships being built.

Here are five simple markers that I believe show a certain quality in relationships between older believers and college-age people:

1. The frequency and consistency with which the pair meets together one-on-one. If they're meeting frequently on their own, without any prodding from others, then it shows that each of them sees the value in the relationship. If there isn't consistency, then it's paramount that we figure out why. It might be a matter of schedules, or it might be that the two people just don't click for some reason. Either way, this is when we can step in and help cultivate that relationship.

2. The college-age person seeks *spiritual* wisdom from the older adult on her own. If this is the case, it says the younger person sees value in this relationship. It also likely suggests that the older believer feels confident in his or her spiritual direction. If this isn't happening, then we may need to equip the older believer or perhaps help the younger one to see the value of someone older investing in her spiritual life.

3. The college-age person knows where the dishes are in the older believer's kitchen. This shows a particular level of intimacy in the relationship, which takes time to develop, of course.

4. The college-age person can drop by the home of an older believer uninvited. This again shows an intimacy and comfort level in the relationship that indicates quality.

5. The college-age person's pursuit of an older believer's counsel in everyday life circumstances. College-age people are thinking

through all sorts of things. If they're seeking the advice of the older believer in their life's direction, educational pursuits, job concerns, or any other daily issues—again, this shows us something about this relationship.

Since it's relational connections we're working toward, measuring the quality of relationship is critical. Not every relationship will have all of these outcomes, of course. But these five points provide something for us to work toward.

BRINGING IT TOGETHER

Helping people process their age-stage issues and cultivate intergenerational relationships are the two factors I've begun leaning on to help me determine both my direction in ministry, as well as how I measure our effectiveness. But focusing on these mentor relationships doesn't take away from the need to focus on a personal relationship with Christ or relationships with other believers. In fact by addressing age-stage issues from a biblical perspective, we're cultivating a deeper personal relationship with Christ (hopefully!). And Christ himself said the world will know we are his disciples by our love for one another (John 13:34). So it's by cultivating loving relationships with other believers that our mission to reach the world is even possible.

Now that we know the role of the ministry and have some practical elements for measuring success (or failure), we can begin discussing what we need to *do*. I'm sure you have some unanswered questions and want more clarity. So in the next chapter we'll look at developing a job description that helps us fulfill our role and work toward some of these outcomes.

THE BOTTOM LINE

- The role of a college ministry is one of assimilation: Helping people move from relational connections in student life to relational connections in the adult life of our churches.

- College-age life is an *in-between* stage, and those who are in this stage need loving mentor voices to help them navigate through five specific pursuits: Identity, intimacy, meaning, pleasure, and truth. These relationships are also a crucial aspect for achieving our goal above.

- We can measure the success of our ministry by (1) how we help college-age people in and through their age-stage issues, and (2) the quality of relationships that college-age people have with older believers.

NOTES:

CHAPTER 3

DEVELOPING A JOB DESCRIPTION (THAT FITS OUR GOALS)

A few years back I started CollegeLeader, a nonprofit organization focused on helping church-based leaders in ministry to college-age people by providing training, resources, and networking. We recently did a little research project where we asked people who are currently working in college ministry to send us their job descriptions. We used all the typical channels to get the word out: Blog, Twitter, social networks, and our newsletter. On the first day, we received more than 100 job descriptions from churches of various sizes in all different regions of the country. It was fun to look through the responses.

Our goal in doing this was simply to see what leaders of college ministries were being asked to do. It was very interesting and insightful. Although the descriptions used unique terms, they all covered a few common areas. For instance most included something about being responsible for a *weekly gathering* or service. I read a lot of phrases like, "Create and develop weekly gatherings that will include biblical teaching and fellowship for college and young adults." This is obviously a very normal—and in many ways vital—aspect of our ministries. It also shows the importance that churches put on making sure that college-age people can connect with each other on a regular basis. But what we do during these gathering times will be a major factor in our long-term effectiveness. I'd personally love to see more specifics in this area of the job descriptions. So in the job description included later in this chapter, I'll add what issues we need to focus on and why.

Most descriptions also mentioned something in regard *to campus ministry,* but the descriptions were very ambiguous. One positive element is that most referred to campus ministry as outreach. College campuses ought to be considered a mission field. Each campus is unique and requires us to reach out to those involved on the campus. (See chapter 17 for more on this.) But as pleased as I was to see some of the missional perspectives,

I was also troubled by the emphasis some churches had. One of them actually stated that the purpose of their campus outreach was to promote the different worship services of their church. In other words the goal is to get people from college campuses to come to the church services. Having college-age people come to our church services isn't a bad thing, but what happens after they do? Who takes it from there? Maybe this church has a strategy for integrating these younger people into the life of their church.

> Most college ministry job descriptions include references to weekly gatherings, campus ministry, and discipleship but lack specifics that get to the heart of what's truly needed in college ministry.

But I'm pretty sure the other staff members' job descriptions wouldn't include assimilating college-age people. This misses the heart of what's truly needed. And I understand that because I've been there.

A third common aspect I saw among the descriptions was something about *discipleship*. A lot of them required the leader to personally take on a certain number of people, usually three to four. And most included something about organizing college-age small groups as well. These are both very good things to include on a job description, but they leave more ambiguity than I'd like to see. What's the goal with those three or four people? Are those to be your ministry leaders or just anybody you click with? If, as the leader, you personally take three or four people under your wing, then what about the rest of them? Don't they need someone speaking into their lives as well? If they do, what's our role in making sure that happens? And if we have small groups, what do they focus on?

There are a whole slew of questions we could be asking. And I understand that most churches hire someone—or appoint a volunteer—who's supposed to answer many of these questions alone. But if you're anything like I was when I started, answering any of the above questions is a challenge. I probably would've come up with something off the cuff, but nothing based on experience. So in this chapter I'd like to help overcome the ambiguity in these areas.

INTENTIONALITY IN DIRECTION

I've already shared a little about how I knew nothing about where to start, what to do, or where to put my focus. This was partly because I didn't have a job description to give me direction. I was basically hired to *start something* and was expected to write my own description. This certainly wasn't bad—

at least our church wanted a ministry to college-age people and was willing to put the finances behind it. And I was completely supported by the staff, pastor, and elders. They believed in this ministry—even though, like me, they had no idea what that *really* meant or what it would look like.

After we'd gotten things going at Cornerstone, I received a ton of emails from people seeking advice for their own ministries. I sat there at my computer like a deer caught in headlights, wondering how to respond. The most common questions were things like, "Where do I start?" Some were even more ambiguous, "We're starting a ministry. Do you have any thoughts?" I tried to help people the best I could, but I didn't know what I was doing. Since then I've been able to identify the things we were doing that proved to have a lasting impact. But at the time I didn't have the vision, skills, or experience to distinguish between the good and the best—and certainly not to the point where I could articulate it to others in one concise email.

So in the remainder of this chapter I'd like to give you eight specific things that have proven to be effective in my ministry over the last 12 years. Remember, we want to work toward accomplishing two things:

1. Help people process their age-stage issues

2. Cultivate quality relationships between college-age people and older, maturing believers

We focus on these two because they're crucial aspects for moving people toward maturity. And by doing so we meet college-age people where they are as well as provide connection to the church as a whole for, hopefully, the remainder of their lives.

The other key point to remember is that these are universal regardless of location, church size, position, or budget. Of course if you're hired to serve full time, you'll be able to pour more time into them. But even if you work full time at another job, you can do these things. Sure, the scale you work with will be different, but what we need to focus on remains the same whether you're volunteering with 10 people or working full time with hundreds.

> What we need to focus on remains the same whether you're volunteering with 10 people or working full time with hundreds.

THE JOB DESCRIPTION

Imagine you were just hired at a church and asked to write your own job description. The following are the points I'd include, as well as my explanation of the importance of each one. This may be longer than what you'd write, and at first glance it may seem overwhelming. But implementing these things can actually be very simple, as long as we stay focused and measure our effectiveness properly. In the next chapter I'll break it down and describe where to start with each area.

Job Description Summary

1. Learn and understand age-stage issues.

2. Personally disciple college-age people.

3. Help cultivate a heart in older believers for younger people.

4. Create bridges for the building of intergenerational relationships.

5. Provide direction for mentorships.

6. Create a gathering point.

7. Develop self-feeders.

8. Develop a relationship with campus leaders.

EIGHT RESPONSIBILITIES OF A COLLEGE-MINISTRY LEADER

1. Learn and Understand Age-Stage Issues

You must have a basic understanding of the issues that college-age people face on a daily basis and stay current through books, articles, and possibly seminars relevant to the topic. (I devoted six chapters to these issues in my previous book, *College Ministry 101*, and I've provided an overview of them in Chapter 5 of this book.) Or start learning about them by asking college-age people the questions I suggest in chapter 10. As leaders, we need to not only understand these issues, but also be able to articulate them—at least to some degree. The degree of our understanding will be the degree to which we can help guide others toward biblically mature conclusions.

Regardless of where you begin, the more you seek understanding, the more effective you'll be in addressing the areas that college-age people are in the midst of processing.

2. Personally Disciple College-Age People

This is a critical aspect for a couple of reasons. First, this is a command for each of us. Our biblical command isn't to run a program; it's to disciple people. And although a program might be a piece of that, it's important to make the distinction. Second, the more you personally help college-age people through their life issues, the more you'll be able to help other leaders do the same. Your experience is going to be critical for the long-term effectiveness of ministry to college age people in your church. There's a reason why states demand that therapists log thousands of hours counseling people before they issue them a license. The more you practice and experience it hands-on, the more likely you are to increase your long-term effectiveness.

As Jesus did with a few select people, we must allow college-age people to see our lives. Just spend time with them. When Jesus looked at his disciples at the end of Matthew 28, he told them to make disciples. All they knew about discipleship was what they'd personally experienced with Jesus. They walked into and out of circumstances with him. Jesus let them into his life to the point where they could see him act and react in everyday life circumstances. They were free to ask questions, doubt, and learn. That was *discipleship* in the mind of Jesus. So when Jesus told his disciples to go and make disciples, they certainly would *not* have walked away thinking they needed to have a weekly meeting and go through a book together! So when I list discipleship as a part of the job description, I mean it as Jesus did it: Through life, not weekly meetings.

Remember, our goal is to make sure that college-age people are connected to the adult life of our churches. This doesn't negate them from being a part of church-sponsored adult events, but their connection to the lives of people *outside* of church-organized events is even more important.

The key isn't the number of people we disciple, but the quality of the relationships we have and are able to cultivate in others. This is why I didn't place a number on it. At the most Jesus personally discipled 12 people. And it could even be argued that he focused on as few as three or four. Even one person would be sufficient for us—if the focus is on quality. I'd recommend that you choose to disciple either the people God has uniquely placed on your heart or those you see as having the most potential of leading others.

3. Help Cultivate a Heart in Older Believers for Younger People

Second Timothy 2:2 (for men) and Titus 2:3-5 (for women) command older believers to initiate mentor-like relationships with younger believers. It's important to remember that this is a command, not a suggestion. So part of our job needs to be helping older believers embrace their God-given responsibility. And obviously this requires us to build relationships with older adults in the church.

We could try to mass-produce this process by putting together a class in the hope of communicating God's desire for older believers to invest in younger ones. But it's far more effective to do this in the context of our own relationships. There are some important facets of this, so I've devoted all of chapters 7 and 8 to this issue.

4. Create Bridges for the Building of Intergenerational Relationships

If the role of our ministry is to bridge people from adolescent life to adult life, then our ministry must be intentional in this. If we're personally allowing college-age people into our lives and helping older adults do the same, then we are creating natural bridges. Truthfully there doesn't have to be any more than this. So if your church doesn't have a college ministry budget, you're limited in terms of time, or maybe you know only two college-age people, you can still be effective in ministry.

But if there *is* more to your college ministry, be sure that everything revolves around this issue. If your ministry or church is doing retreats, mission trips, justice projects, or other events, take advantage of these opportunities to build relational bridges. There are very practical ways to do this, so I've devoted later chapters to individual avenues of ministry to help you be sure they're all working toward your long-term goals. But building bridges for intergenerational relationships is a must on your job description.

5. Provide Direction for Mentorships

As the leader you'll need to help those who are mentoring college-age people in a variety of ways. Nothing teaches people quite like a living example, so most of this will be accomplished through your modeling what you want them to do. Sometimes you may need to give advice on how they can help someone, help them gain deeper understanding into normal college-age issues, or just encourage them to keep things simple. But the most crucial aspect is helping them feel confident in their role in the life of a college-age person.[3] (See chapter 7 for more on this.)

6. Create a Gathering Point

While the primary need and desire of college-age people is to be connected to the church as a whole, there is value in their building relationships with each other. Putting together some type of gathering point where college-age people can be around their peers is important. It doesn't matter if it's in a home over a meal or at a larger gathering on the church campus. But, perhaps even most importantly, this is another avenue through which age-specific issues can be addressed in a variety of ways. We can teach a series on each one, or we can teach through books of the Bible, bringing application points back to each of the five areas they're pursuing. Creativity allows for anything, really, but the focus of this time is twofold: Building peer relationships and addressing age-stage issues.

7. Develop Self-Feeders

This is a natural part of discipleship, but I believe it's important to list it as a separate responsibility. It's impossible for a person to work toward maturity in Christ without being able to study Scripture and hear from God on their own. Sometimes we wrongly assume that since people know *about* Scripture, they must also know how to get truth *out of* Scripture.

I've seen hundreds and hundreds of young adults who were raised in the church and know *about* Scripture. They've been taught doctrine and can often regurgitate it. But sadly, most people sitting in our churches don't feel confident studying Scripture for themselves. And if our goal is to move people toward maturity, then this must be a part of our job description. We can teach on this topic in our gathering points, we can design our small groups around this concept (which I recommend and will explain in chapter 11), and we can encourage those who are mentoring college-age people to help in this area. But again, this must start with us leading by example and letting our experience flow into the lives of others.

---

3. I coauthored a book titled *The Slow Fade: Why You Matter in the Story of Twentysomethings* that's designed to be given to the older adults in your church for this exact purpose.

8. Develop a Relationship with Campus Leaders

There are very few campuses that don't have someone who's already trying to reach students in some fashion. But the disconnection between church-based and campus-based ministries is great—and horrifying. If we're going to be effective in understanding what college-age people deal with every day, then we have to be in touch with their lives. And for many of them, their lives are on campus. Campus ministry workers can be some of your greatest resources. With the long term in mind, college students need a connection to a church, and that makes you vital to their ministry. Without that connection, the chances of them disconnecting entirely from the body of Christ after they graduate are high.

Again, this might seem like a daunting task for you if you work full time elsewhere, but it doesn't have to be. Start by looking for one person working on one campus. In chapter 17 I'll talk more about this and give some suggestions for where to start if you don't already have any connections with campus leaders.

KEEPING IT SIMPLE

If you go back through each of these responsibilities, you'll see that they are universally necessary to be effective in college ministry. And they're universal regardless of context, your position, and the size of the ministry budget. (The one exception might be a very small rural church with no campus nearby, and where all students leave to attend college. I've devoted chapter 18 to how to continue ministry to those types of college students.) If we keep it simple and measure our effectiveness beyond numerical attendance, then we're on our way to having an effective and sustainable ministry to college-age people.

The fact is that if your job description is purely programmatic, you'll miss the central responsibilities of a ministry leader. You can have hundreds of college-age people coming to a gathering point and still be missing most, if not all, of the above aspects. My prayer for you is that you'll keep focused on what's truly necessary, start off with a

> If we keep it simple and measure our effectiveness beyond numerical attendance, then we're on our way to having an effective and sustainable ministry to college-age people.

proper balance, and go one step at a time as you hit each of these areas. And getting started on the right foot is what I hope to help you do in the next chapter.

THE BOTTOM LINE

- Everything in the job description should work toward the goals of helping people process their age-stage issues and developing a certain quality in relationships with older adults.

- Each of the eight responsibilities listed are universal to college ministry regardless of context, your position, or the size of the ministry budget.

NOTES:

CHAPTER 4

YOUR FIRST 90 DAYS IN COLLEGE MINISTRY

I was attending one of Youth Specialties' (YS) National Youth Workers' Conventions in Sacramento, California, when I first met Mike Yaconelli. I, of course, knew *of* him—he was an author and the president and cofounder of YS, but I'd never met him. As we walked past each other in a hallway, I stopped him and introduced myself. I told him I'd recently been hired by a church to start a college ministry (part time), and I was wondering why there weren't any seminars at the Convention for that sort of thing. He told me the YS staff had been talking about it, but they just hadn't put anything together yet. So I let him know there was at least one guy out there who could really use some help (me). We talked for a couple more minutes, and that was the end of that conversation.

When the next year's Convention came around, part of my role at the church was now overseeing the student ministries. So we brought our staff and key volunteers to the Convention. One afternoon I was walking down a hallway when I saw Mike again. As we passed each other, I stopped him and reintroduced myself. I said, "Hey, Mike. My name is Chuck Bomar. I know you don't remember me, but I talked to you at the Convention last year..." He cut me off right there and said, "COLLEGE MINISTRY! You asked me about college ministry, right?!" He remembered me? Crazy, weird . . . and divine.

I let him know, once again, that I'd come looking for a college ministry seminar to attend, but they still didn't have one. I had a bit of sarcasm in my tone—okay, maybe a lot—but I just wanted him to know there was at least one person out there who'd attend a college ministry seminar. I also let him know that I thought there was a greater need out there, and I shared about some other youth pastor friends of mine who were also struggling for some direction in their college ministries. So we talked for a few minutes, and he asked me a few questions about my ministry—what our needs were and how I thought YS could help those of us in college ministry.

Then he suddenly cut me off again, grabbed my hand, and told me to come with him. So I followed him through the twists and turns of the hallways until we arrived in the main session room. Mike took me backstage and introduced me to Mark Oestreicher, who was vice president of YS at the time. As I was shaking hands with Marko, Yac said, "Marko, Chuck is going to lead a seminar on college ministry at next year's Conventions!"

I was confused.

Humbled, but totally confused.

This wasn't the reason I'd approached him, nor was I in any position to teach a seminar! I told him there was no way I could do that. I believe my exact words were, "What?! No way, man. I'm the guy who needs a seminar to attend!" I'm pretty sure that didn't give Marko any confidence in me, but it was the truth. I was trying to figure out what to do myself, and I didn't have any idea as to why I was doing what I was doing. But Yac clearly disagreed. He said I knew more than I thought I did, and then he added, "Plus, you have an entire year to prepare!"

I'd always heard that Mike did crazy things, but this was WAY over the top and could probably be better classified as *insane*. This might have caused some to question the integrity of the entire organization. It certainly would have if they'd known how aimless I was.

The beauty of this encounter was that it forced me to continue thinking through college ministry. I became much more intentional about asking questions and seeking answers—for myself. So based on the thousands of hours I've spent asking and answering questions since that day I talked with Yac, I want to give you a sort of road map for your first 90 days in ministry. I did some of these things myself, and I would do them again. But I didn't embrace some of what I'll describe until later in my ministry.

So I hope you can learn from my experiences—successes and failures. The way you start your ministry will set the trajectory for the long term, so doing a few things in the beginning can save you a lot of heartache in the future. Ah, the things I wish I'd known!

STARTING OFF RIGHT

I remember the first time I went into my pastor's office with a PowerPoint slide (similar to Figure 1.1 in chapter 2) illustrating what I thought was the role of college ministry in our church. He agreed with the overall direction, but neither of us knew what to do to get there. Sure, I had some ideas for how to connect college-age people with the adult life in our church. But many of them proved to be not as effective as I thought. Today is, of course, a little different. I've learned some things the hard way and continue to learn, but I'm definitely sure of a few things that I'd devote my time to if I were starting a college ministry from scratch.

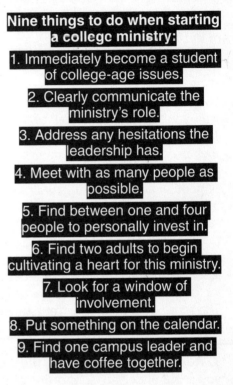

Nine things to do when starting a college ministry:

1. Immediately become a student of college-age issues.
2. Clearly communicate the ministry's role.
3. Address any hesitations the leadership has.
4. Meet with as many people as possible.
5. Find between one and four people to personally invest in.
6. Find two adults to begin cultivating a heart for this ministry.
7. Look for a window of involvement.
8. Put something on the calendar.
9. Find one campus leader and have coffee together.

So here is a short list of things I'd recommend doing in the beginning of your ministry. Depending on the amount of time you have to invest in the ministry, it may seem daunting or overly simplistic. And, just so you know, there is no magic number to the "90 days" in this chapter title. All I'm really saying is that these are things that need to be focused on in the beginning.

Start Something

If you sent me an email asking where you should start or what to do as you start something for college-age people, these are nine things I'd suggest that you make sure to do:

1. Immediately become a student of college-age issues. When I started in ministry, I couldn't find any resources that directly applied to what I was doing! Some of this was due to my narrow searches, but much of it was because there was a severe lack of resources available for church-based ministries.[4] It's not important to understand everything right now; you just need to be a student of the people you work with. Starting somewhere and slowly learning is going to be a crucial aspect of your ministry. Thankfully some resources are readily available now.

2. Clearly communicate the ministry's role. This is perhaps the most critical thing you must do in the beginning. It's important that you're not alone in this understanding, especially when it comes to the leadership under which you serve. In a sense your biggest responsibility from early on is casting the vision of the ministry. This, without question, begins with the leadership of the church.

Your first priority is to make sure they understand what you're doing and why you're doing it. If you begin moving too fast and before the leaders of the church understand the role of the ministry, then the measurements they use to evaluate your ministry could be totally unfair. This is especially true if you're in a church where other measurements are based on numbers of people. Communicating your role as the assimilation of people will help others keep realistic expectations and provide proper measurements. You can even walk them through some of the ways in which you're going to measure the effectiveness by using this book as a starting point.

Also, communicating the role doesn't have to stop with the leadership. In fact it shouldn't. It's best to casually talk about it with all of your friends. The more people in your church who understand what the needs are and what the role of the ministry is, the more sustainable the ministry will be.

3. Address any hesitations the leadership has. Even when the leaders you serve under are supportive of your starting something for college-age people, they're likely to have some underlying questions. You'll want to be prepared and clear in your own mind if or when these inquiries come up. So I want to briefly address some general hesitations that I've seen in leaders over the years:

- *Campus ministries are already involved with college-age people, so what role do we play?* First, campus ministries are usually good at connecting peer relationships but not intergenerational ones. This is one distinction and benefit of a church. Second, not every college-

---

4. I've already mentioned in the previous chapters some potential resources you could use, and I know this book is a step in that direction for you as well. But over the years, I've found some resources that are helpful. Go to www.CollegeLeader.org/resources-links and you'll find some recommended links for resources and reading—free Internet-based resources, as well as books I'd recommend. You don't have to agree with everything (I know I don't), but they can be a help to you in your ministry.

age person attends a school where campus ministries exist. And third, not all college-age people attend school.

- *We don't have enough money in the budget.* A budget isn't necessary if everything is focused on relational connections.

- *We're not located in a college town.* An estimated 75 percent of 18-to-24 year olds don't attend a four-year college full time. This suggests there are at least some people in this age-stage living in your area. And the age-stage issues are the same, regardless of whether or not someone attends a major university.

- *Our church is so old and it doesn't appeal to younger people.* This might be true if you're looking at it from a church service (or programmatic) perspective. But the needs and desires of college-age people are much simpler. Remember, they desire relational connection. And most would love another "grandma" in their lives. Just ask them!

- *We've tried this before and it didn't work.* Well, maybe you tried putting together a programmatic college ministry, rather than concentrating on ministering to them as individuals. Trying a different approach and recruiting older believers to be involved in a one-on-one approach could be worth a try.

- *We're not sure it's worth the investment; many will leave and go to other churches.* Your church probably supports missionaries who don't attend or tithe to your church, so consider viewing the college-age person in a similar manner. The only difference is that investing in college-age people doesn't require any of your budget, yet it has the same (and possibly greater) long-term benefits.

- *We can't pay anyone for this position.* Although a paycheck would be great, it's not necessary. Having an effective ministry to college-age people requires helping older believers embrace their responsibility of investing in younger believers. All we need to get started is one adult who will lead by example.

- *There aren't enough college-age people to do something.* That might be true if we're looking at putting money and other resources into a programmatic approach. But all we're talking about is ministering to one person at a time—individually. The point is not to reach an entire generation but to get older believers to invest in one person.

Plus, the lack of college-age people should be *the* reason you do something! How many junior high students would be involved in your church if you had nothing for them?

4. Meet with as many people as possible. Spend as much time with college-age people as possible—meet with them one-on-one, if you can. Get to know them and allow them to get to know you. Through these times you'll find some with huge leadership potential, some who desperately need you to speak truth, some who are hurting, and others who don't even believe in Jesus. This will give you a great feel for where people are at and what their needs are, and it might even show you where to start.

5. Find between one and four people to personally invest in. You may already be investing in a few college-age people; but if not, start now. It's crucial. You'll need other adults to help in this venture, and it's very important that you model this for them.

I remember calling the four people in our "database" and meeting with them. I was just trying to get to know them. That's it. And it's one thing that I'd do the same way if I had it to do over again. Relationships take time to build and the time is worth spending. There isn't any rush, but don't put off finding a few people to pursue in order to get to know them better. Ideally you want to spend one-on-one time with these people but, if time is limited, start out meeting all together. The format isn't important. The key is allowing at least one person into your life.

Looking back at the two measurements we discussed in chapter 2 (processing age-stage issues and older believers investing in the lives of younger ones) and working toward those in this relationship is a great place to start. When I met with people in the beginning, I didn't have anything to work toward. Some of this was very healthy because I didn't have an agenda of any sort. But just getting to know a few people and allowing them to get to know you (and possibly your family) is something you need to implement immediately.

One encouragement is to go into these relationships with an open hand. These individuals may not be the people you personally invest in for the long term. Instead, you may find that another adult is a better fit for that person. That's okay. There doesn't need to be a long-term strategy for each relationship. You just need to start assimilating them into your life first, and then take it one day at a time.

6. Find two adults to begin cultivating a heart for this ministry. Most likely you know at least two friends you can encourage to invest in a college-age person. Sharing your passion for college-age people, how they actually speak into your life, and even your own convictions about the biblical commands to invest in younger people is one of the best things you can do. I cannot emphasize this part of your ministry enough. A major part of your role is being the bridge builder for intergenerational relationships, so encouraging older believers is perhaps the most practical thing I can encourage you to do. This way, when college-age people bring up various issues they're dealing with, you already know an adult or two with whom you can connect them. (I'll describe practical ways of going about this and natural connecting points in chapter 6.)

You see, your role is really about creating a culture in your church. You cannot program this, nor can you sustain the depth of relationship with every person. It takes others besides you, and it has to happen one person at a time. Time spent with older believers will allow you to share your heart and vision for the ministry. And the more people who catch those things, the more sustainable the ministry will be.

7. Look for a window of involvement. College-age people want to be involved in our churches and particularly a part of solutions. Many of them have insights and concerns that can really be a benefit to our churches. The problem is they're rarely given a platform to voice those things, which is why we must advocate for them. All leaders in every church are thinking through something. In any way possible, find windows of opportunity for college-age people to be involved in those processes. If you're aware of something their voice could speak to, be their ambassador! Share with those leaders about the value of college-age people being involved. We want and need college-age people to be a part of these types of things. Not only will the church benefit from their input, but also it allows college-age people to have a sense of belonging. And this is crucial!

8. Put something on the calendar. I had a barbeque at my house, but you could do anything. Just make sure it's relaxed and relational. Don't worry about having a formal study of any kind or an extended prayer time. These things will come naturally in time. Remember, college-age people are seeking relational connections, not necessarily another study. Another study could actually be a turn-off for many. And as I'll point out in the chapters to come, this is anything but shallow. Relationships are a key aspect in formulating an identity, so helping them connect with other believers—starting with their peers—is crucial to our ministry.

But don't lose sight of the long-term vision of a deeper connection to the church. You can begin by taking full advantage of this first meeting time by inviting a friend to join you. Maybe you have a barbeque at your house, and you just invite a friend (or couple) to come and hang out as well. Their role is to be there, hang out, and get to know someone. That's it. By doing something as simple as this, you're beginning to set the trajectory of your ministry.

Start by getting something on the calendar. This could turn into a bi-weekly or monthly thing you do. It doesn't really matter as long as it's relational and you're focused on bridging relationships. This could potentially become the only gathering point for your ministry, and over time you can begin to have a time of teaching or discussion. Just take it one day at a time and focus on building relationships first, not programs.

9. Find one campus leader and have coffee together. If you live next to a campus of any kind, seek out one leader and schedule a time to get together with that person. Your goal is relationship building. That's it. You can let them know your focus on the ministry and even tell them you're working hard at cultivating a heart in the older believers to include college students in their lives. You might be surprised at how excited that campus leader could be about this idea. Regardless, the important thing is that you connect at least one time with someone.

TAKING IT SLOW

Looking at these all at once can be daunting. But I want to encourage you to remember that these are just ideas to begin with. You don't need to tackle everything right now. It's beginning your focus on things like these that's really going to help your long-term effectiveness. Once you see the benefit and simplicity of this approach, you won't feel like you need to do anything else. Trust me on that. You might eventually do more, but there's no rush, no hurry...and no *need*. Just take it one day at a time.

Maybe the first week you simply schedule an appointment with your pastor to begin the conversation about the role of this ministry. Maybe it's not until the following week that you're able to sit down and figure out a few college-age people you want to be intentional with. Whatever the case, it's

You're not seeking to grow a ministry—you're looking to develop a sustainable culture in which college-age people feel loved and a part of the church as a whole. And that takes time.

fine. Just focus on one thing at a time, one person at a time, and take it slow. You're not seeking to grow a ministry—you're looking to develop a sustainable culture in which college-age people feel loved and a part of the church as a whole. And that takes time. I'll share much more on this in the next two chapters.

THE BOTTOM LINE

- The things you do in the beginning of your ministry will set the long-term trajectory.

- Make sure you understand the people you're ministering to and what you're trying to accomplish, and then clearly communicate those things to other leaders in your church.

- Start investing in a few college-age people and find others to do the same.

- Take it slowly, one day at a time. You're in this for the long haul, so there's no rush.

NOTES:

CHAPTER 5

UNDERSTANDING COLLEGE-AGE ISSUES—AN OVERVIEW

....

Ashley is an amazing girl.[5] She's 23 years old and has one of those personalities you can't help but like and enjoy being around. Some people just seem to have everything going for them. Everybody likes them—they're intelligent, they're witty, they stand out in a crowd, and they're just a joy to be around. That's Ashley.

But she's also just like other college-age people who are stuck between a free-spirited adolescent world and that of, well, adulthood. Ashley looks to adulthood as a time of stability, which she desires. But for her it's also a scary time in which all spontaneity and world-changing possibilities disappear. She has a deep-rooted passion to change the world, yet at the same time she has this inner turmoil to find a steady and consistent place in society as an adult. She's normal . . . and in between.

She recently quit a great-paying job to go to Africa for four months and serve in an orphanage. Now she's back in the States and wondering what the next year or so will bring for her. On one side she's thinking about going to another country for a year and teaching English, while on the other she's thinking she might want to stay in one place for a while, get a job, and settle down a bit. I talk to her about these decisions every once in a while, and I can honestly say I'm not sure where she'll land. In fact I wouldn't be surprised if she ends up doing something entirely different from what's being considered at this moment.

Some might think she's lost, indecisive, and just needs to choose something and stick with it. I'd suggest differently. I believe she ought to continue exploring, having different experiences, and discovering. I'm not suggesting that she do this forever, nor am I condoning a life of aimless self-pleasure. I am, however, suggesting that she not get sucked into the all-too-powerful pressure to settle down in adulthood before she discovers who she is.

---

5. Her name has been changed to protect her privacy.

Now is her opportunity to really get a sense of who she is, embrace her identity in Christ, and *then* find a place where she fits in society. The only alternative is for her to substitute who she *actually* is for a role in normal society—potentially appeasing other adults who are pressuring her to join their world.

The college-age stage of life should be a time of exploration and self-discovery. We can view this as being flaky, inconsistent, and undisciplined. Or we can view it as a time of identity formulation. I choose the latter.

> The college-age stage of life should be a time of exploration and self-discovery.

IDENTITY—A SEARCH FOR SELF

At first glance it might seem as though I'm a free-for-all advocate. Not really. I'm not in favor of anyone floating through life with no direction or motivation. I just don't believe the answer is to find a steady job somewhere. Somehow in our culture there's a pressure to give in to that idea. The pursuit of a career is certainly one way God uses to lead some people in self-discovery. But the cultural pressure to find a career and the promise of discovering one's identity and fulfillment in that position can be deceptive and destructive. Not only do I believe it's potentially devastating to a person's identity formulation, but I also happen to believe it's unbiblical. The more I'm around college-age people, the more I recognize the health of their taking time to discover themselves beyond the things, relationships, or career paths that are found on earth.

No part of Scripture leads us to believe that our identity is, or should be, found in earthly things or roles. In fact, it says quite the opposite. Paul spends the first three chapters of Ephesians talking about how our identity is found in the spiritual blessings of Christ. In his first letter written to those living under an oppressive Roman emperor, Peter spends at least the first two chapters describing their *actual* identity as being completely imperishable. He even goes so far as to call them *sojourners*, meaning they're simply passing through this world. This earth is not their home.

I could go on and on about how Scripture talks about this concept, quoting passage after passage. Yet there is literally nothing in God's Word that allows us to believe that our identity as Christians is in this world—or even tied to it. Sure, we live in the world and we each have a role here. But as believers we aren't defined by circumstances. Instead, we're to be who we are *regardless* of the circumstances. Even so, for college-age people—and for most of us—determining who they are beyond these things is extremely difficult.

Too many people allow themselves to choose their identities through some circumstance (such as a career or relationship) before they really find themselves. And I don't want to be a part of that—or pressure someone else to fall into that trap. This is why I'm not pushing Ashley to just find something and stick with it. She's not finished discovering who she is in Christ yet, which is far more important to discover than any career path.

As I said earlier, the pursuit of identity is not an issue—it's *the* issue as we guide young adults through our college-age ministries. Understanding this is of utmost importance. Of course the process of self-discovery is, at some level, a lifelong process. But it's in full throttle between the ages of 18 and 25. Some will continue this search into their upper twenties, and still others will take even longer to figure it out. This is why we need to be involved. As spiritual leaders we must be able to lead spiritually. And this leading starts by helping college-age people find and embrace their spiritual identities. If we Christians don't find our

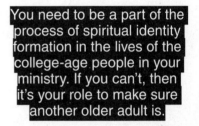

You need to be a part of the process of spiritual identity formation in the lives of the college-age people in your ministry. If you can't, then it's your role to make sure another older adult is.

identity and belonging in Christ and within the body of Christ, we lose who we *actually* are. Our *true* identity is found only in a biblical understanding of who God made us to be in Christ.[6] A loss of true spiritual identity results in a loss of our role in the world.

This process of self-discovery can include a ton of internal confusion. But we don't have to be psychiatrists to guide it. We just have to know people, spend time with them, and help them think biblically about who they are. As a college-ministry leader you need to be a part of this process. If you can't, then it's your role to make sure another older adult is. College-age people desperately need someone to help them through the intellectual and emotional gymnastics that this discovery process entails. The following are some areas to focus on as you start your ministry.[7]

---

6. This is what I call the "Theologian stage," and it's where we want to guide people. See chapter 2 of *College Ministry 101* for more on this.

7. More information about these issues can be found in my book *College Ministry 101.*

Intimacy

Relationships are vital to college-age people. The more they have, the better. And if they're deeper and more intimate than most relationships, then that's better still. I'm not speaking of sexual things, of course, but of depth. College-age people have a tremendous desire for intimate relationships. They long to know someone and to be known. The more they discover about other people, the more they discover about themselves. And this is why relationships are pursued with vigor and why we ought to make sure they're cultivated in our ministries.

College-age people go through a natural and normal process in relationships that I refer to as *differentiation and integration*. This isn't necessarily a conscious process, but for some it is. College-age people are very much in tune with others. They'll notice characteristics and traits in people that they personally desire and respect or find repulsive and don't respect. They then differentiate what they see in others from what they believe is in themselves. This differentiation is a very normal part of relationships, and it's instrumental in helping self-discovery.

We've all been around someone who's passionate to the point that it makes us want to be more passionate, too. We notice something desirable in someone else, differentiate that with ourselves, and then move to integrate that characteristic into our own lives. We see this all the time in our interns. For instance when someone is learning to teach they usually begin by mimicking someone else. They've noticed the things a particular teacher does, desire that same attribute (probably because they found it effective or intriguing), and begin integrating it into their own teaching style. College-age people do this all the time, and it's a necessary process in formulating an identity.

So if they go through this process of differentiation and integration anyway, why not guide it? We can take what normally happens and assist the process of identity formation by putting certain people in their lives. And we can be very intentional about the adults we expose them to—spiritually maturing adults who have Christlike characteristics and are willing to allow a college-age person to get to know them. This is a simple, inexpensive, yet highly effective way of guiding one of the most important developmental processes a person can go through: Identity formulation.

Meaning

Stephen and I were talking the other day about his relationship with his dad.[8] His parents are divorced, and his dad raised him. As the vice president of a company, his dad is considered to be very successful in the business world, and he's been pushing Stephen to figure out what he's going to do with his life. He feels that choosing a career path is one of the most important decisions Stephen can make during this time of his life. Stephen is going to have responsibilities to take care of, so figuring this out is very meaningful for his dad. We can certainly understand this viewpoint to some degree.

On the other hand, Stephen's perspective on this process couldn't be more different. For him future responsibilities are just that—*future* responsibilities. And working toward fulfilling those now seems ridiculous since he doesn't even know what he *wants* to do yet. What's meaningful for Stephen is determining what he wants first. This takes a lot of time to figure out, and one of the—for lack of a better term—stepping-stones to this realization is self-discovery. The more Stephen knows about himself, the more he can decipher what he wants to do for the rest of his life.

The dichotomy between these two perspectives is crucial to understand if you're going to be effective in college ministry. We'll discuss this more in chapter 18, but this is where you and the parents might interface. Tension creeps into Stephen's relationship with his dad over this issue, so it's important that college-ministry leaders understand both sides.

On the one hand we can see the dad's point: Stephen will need to work toward something eventually because one day he'll be an independent adult who must support himself and, potentially, a family. On the other hand we can understand Stephen's hesitancy to jump into something just so he can have a direction. He doesn't want to get stuck doing something that he doesn't like or find meaningful. And in order for him to avoid that catastrophe, he needs to take this process slowly and shouldn't flippantly choose something.

Our role isn't to pick one side over the other but to guide both of them. We need to make sure that people like Stephen are becoming more self-aware, exploring different things, and intentionally thinking through who they are. Making sure they're developing intimate relationships is one way of doing this, but another is simply being a part of their lives—walking with them through job and college degree or major changes, being there when they break up with a longtime girlfriend or boyfriend, seeing them interact with

---

8. His name has been changed to protect his privacy.

someone in need, or possibly allowing them to serve you. It's by knowing them that we can help them discover their own desires. And beyond that—God's desires for them.

The quest for self-fulfillment is a very Western concept. Most of the world's population is struggling just to survive and meet their basic needs, so they don't have that luxury. Seeing this struggle firsthand or through the experiences of others can help college-age people gain perspective on their lives and the choices they face.

The important thing to keep in mind is that they're intentionally thinking through it and we're to help them avoid that aimless float through life. This takes longer for some than others, but being a part of a person's journey as they seek to define what's meaningful can be one of the most rewarding aspects of ministry—especially if we can help them define meaning in the same way that God does. That's when it gets really fun.[9]

> The quest for self-fulfillment is a very Western concept, and a luxury most of the world doesn't have as they struggle to survive and meet basic needs.

PLEASURE

We all seek pleasure. It's normal and in some ways it can even be healthy. But it can also be dangerous. I can't tell you how many people I've worked with over the years who simply do whatever they want, whenever they want, and they don't even think about anyone else. So many college-age people go from one event to another with nothing on their minds but their own desires and newfound freedoms. College-age people are at a point in their lives where they have more freedom from parental influence than ever before, and most of them want to take full advantage of it. It's not a bad thing, but it can be dangerous.

In our ministries we certainly don't want to rob them of this joy and freedom. We can even be a part of it. Some of my best times in ministry have been doing fun—and even stupid—things with college-age people. One time, while on our way to a ski trip in Utah, we stopped off at Caesars Palace in Las Vegas. We were looking for a buffet so we could grab an inexpensive meal when we walked past a huge statue of Caesar. Now, you can't just walk past something like this without taking a picture. So we did. But then we decided that wasn't good enough. Caesar's arms were held out

---

9. There are many more issues that need to be addressed in this pursuit. So for more conversation on this issue, see chapter 4 in *College Ministry 101*.

in a way that suggested he could be holding us in the picture. So I climbed up and made myself comfortable in Caesar's arms, and the others took my picture. That is, until five security guards came up and kicked me out of the casino. *Oops.*

We'll always have fun with people, and I think fun is a very important part of our ministries. But instead of *just* doing things that we personally find pleasing, we can also help college-age people find pleasure in serving others. Jesus says, "It is more blessed to give than to receive."[10] Do you believe that? Really? Do you really believe you'll be more blessed—find more pleasure—by giving to someone else than by receiving? We might know this in theory, but the truth is that few people really believe it. If we did, then we'd probably give a lot more and seek self-pleasure far less.

College-age people, for the most part, don't believe this either. But we can help change their perception by exposing them to the pleasures of serving others. College-age people are some of the most passionate around. They see the needs in the world, and they certainly want to be a part of the solutions. We can take them on mission trips (see chapter 14), do local justice projects, or support national ones—there are so many things we can do.

> Helping college-age people find pleasure in giving and being a part of eternal things is one of the best things we can do to help them embrace their true spiritual identities.

Focusing on helping college-age people find pleasure in giving has to be a very important aspect of our ministries. Helping them find pleasure in being a part of eternal things is one of the best things we can do to help them embrace their true spiritual identities. And when they talk about the joy and pleasure they feel from helping others, we can then tie that into who they really are. Again, it's a very practical way of being a part of and guiding the identity formulation of a person.[11]

Truth

Do I actually believe this, or do I just think *I do because my parents believe it?* Regardless of one's religious upbringing, this is the underlying question that most college-age people are not only asking, but also consciously pursuing the answers. The college-age years are a time of questioning, challenging,

---

10. Acts 20:35

11. For more on this, see chapter 6 in *College Ministry 101.*

and even confusion. But it's a necessary time. In fact so much so that if a college-age person *isn't* asking these questions and challenging themselves, then we need to force it to happen.

Once they're out of their parents' home, pretty much everything they assumed to be true is reevaluated. This process of determining what they personally believe is yet another crucial step in identity formulation. Answering this question is necessary to stand on one's own and allow one's personal beliefs to drive his or her adult life.

Leaders and parents tend to freak out when college-age kids go through this process. We think they're abandoning everything, but it's quite the contrary. While this process might lead them not to embrace some of the same convictions that we have, there is a huge difference between questioning and abandoning.

As leaders it's important to realize that this time of questioning doesn't mean that every belief will be thrown out the window. It just means that every belief needs to be sifted through in order to make it personal. And this is something we need to allow—and sometimes force—to happen. A large part of our role is helping these young adults find their own identities, and faith convictions are certainly a critical part of that.

THE POINT

Okay, this was an extremely brief explanation of the issues. But whether or not you focus on these issues in your ministry will determine whether or not you meet college-age people where they're at in life. And, ultimately, this will determine your success in ministry. This isn't an exhaustive list by any means; but if you miss these core issues, you're going to miss the heart of this ministry. Just remember that everything you do is focused on helping college-age people formulate and embrace their true spiritual identities.

So what does all of this look like? It might mean that you work to connect them in intimate relationships with older godly people so you can indirectly guide their identity formation. Maybe it means you spend two years with someone as they discover what they want in life. It could also mean putting together a ton of service and mission trips to help people discover the beauty of giving to others. Or it could potentially mean that you spend a considerable amount of time talking about faith assumptions one-on-one or in small groups. Whatever the case, everything comes down to helping them think through who they are. And doing this in the context of the church is where the process ought to take place.

THE BOTTOM LINE

- College-age people are sifting through five major issues in life: Identity, intimacy, meaning, pleasure, and truth.

- Every aspect of your ministry should focus on addressing these issues.

- All five issues help form a person's identity, so it's important to guide each area.

NOTES:

CHAPTER 6

PROVIDING A PLACE TO BELONG

Everybody wants to belong.

And it's important that they *do* belong—especially in the context of a church.

I remember talking with Nick just before I moved to Portland to plant our church.[12] We were sitting at a great little breakfast place called Chef Burger in Simi Valley. I know it doesn't *sound* like a great breakfast place, but believe me—it's amazing! It's actually one of my all-time favorites—that and the Greek restaurant…. Man, that's a good one, too.

Anyway, Nick had just graduated from college, and I guess you could say he needed a boost in life. The phase that I refer to as *the morning after college graduation* can be really tough on some people. Many hopes and dreams for what a college degree might bring come crashing down when the post-graduation job prospects are so few. Nick didn't have any life direction, didn't have any luck finding a job, and didn't have much motivation to find one. Not surprisingly he often felt depressed. He was stuck in a rut of living by the minute, completely for himself, and with no sense of belonging in the world.

Nick wanted to meet with me to ask if he could come with my family and me to help with the church plant. There's much more to this situation, but the truth was that he wasn't in a position to *help* us. But I thought we could help him. I remember looking at him at the end of the conversation and letting him know that he could come with us, but I emphasized that he was going to have to put a lot of effort into finding a job and staying involved with people in our church. He agreed and made the decision to move.

This ended up being a huge turning point for him. The most significant thing was being able to be a part of something bigger than himself. In fact

---

12. His name has been changed to protect his privacy.

he was so excited that he packed up and moved a thousand miles away to be a part of that *thing*. But the real beauty was the fact that this *thing* was the church.

> College-age Christians crave belonging in the church, and they want to be a core part of it.

Believe me, college-age Christians crave belonging in the church, and they want to be a core part of it. Some might rant and rave about the institutional side of things (other words might be used), but mostly that's because they don't feel like they belong in that structure.

Nick moved, quickly built some relationships with people, and immediately began his job search. He found a job pretty quickly, and it was one he excelled at. He's a very sharp guy, and he found a place where he was valued and appreciated for what he brought to the company. This was a great step for him for many reasons, but perhaps the most significant was his realization that the workplace is a mission field.

I can't tell you how many times I've seen this same progression. Like Nick, when college-age people find belonging in the church, everything begins to change for them. An important lesson I learned is that allowing people to have a sense of belonging in the church as a whole is what gives them belonging in the world. And I'd even suggest that if we lose our identity among the people of God, we lose our identity in the world.

BELONGING

Recently Nick had another job offer that was very enticing to him. It had a ton of potential for growth, and it immediately started paying 20 percent more than he's currently making. As he thought and prayed through this opportunity, there were all kinds of things he was thinking through. Although he's good at his current job, he's getting a little bored. And with the economy being in a recession, his company is making cutbacks. So that's a concern, too. Therefore this job seemed like a great opportunity for him to try something new, make more money, and potentially dodge a layoff. But he wasn't settled on it for some reason.

Thankfully, because he's connected to older believers in our church, Nick didn't have to think through the decision alone. And he knew that. One night at a random pasta party that a couple in our church hosted, Nick stood in the kitchen and began talking to a guy about this job opportunity.

Before long, Nick had a group of people gathered around him, helping him process this decision. Nick stood there and immediately felt loved, invested in, and like he belonged. He didn't have to make this decision in a vacuum because he was a part of a body of people who could help him think through it. They knew Nick, loved him, and genuinely were invested in his life. In Nick's words, "It was so cool to be able to glean off the wisdom of some older men."

I recently asked Nick to share this experience during a Sunday morning service. He shared how these people helped him think through things with a kind of *spiritual wisdom* (Colossians 1:9-10) that he didn't have quite yet. But he does now! His final decision—and it was *his* decision—was to stay where he was. And the reason he chose to stay was because he felt like his relationships with his co-workers were finally at a point where he could really start speaking into their lives. In fact the other day he told me that if he'd decided to leave, then his ministry with these people would have been compromised. He said, "The only reason I would leave is because it benefits me. And if I left for more money and a better opportunity for myself, I think that would hurt my witness as to what it means to be a Christian."

Wow! I can't tell you how exciting that was for me to hear. What a change!

It's this type of growth that we all long to see in the lives of those we invest in. But the biggest thing is that Nick feels like he belongs to a body of believers who love and support him. It's not just an individual ministry that Nick feels a part of, and it's certainly not just my relationship with him that gives him a sense of belonging. It's his relationship with people in our church body. And it's his belonging in our church that shapes his identity in the world.

THREE RELATIONSHIPS

It's through situations like this that I see how a sense of belonging is found. To gain a sense of belonging, people will look to their relationships with—

- Themselves

- God

- The world (others)

Processing through these relationships is ongoing for all of us, but it's during the college-age years that all three are intensely assessed. People in this age-stage are consciously thinking through the following questions: *Who am I? How am I unique? What do I believe? How do I fit into this place called Earth?*

Answering these questions is vital to finding belonging. Any one of them left unanswered leaves a person in a state of wander and ambiguity. Our role as spiritual leaders, however, is to help people answer these questions through the lens of faith—and give them a safe place to do it.

College-age people are no longer children, but they're not quite adults either. They're in a crucial time of self-discovery, and there are all kinds of factors that play into this. For instance, they're exploring different jobs, majors, relationships, and even beliefs. It all goes back to the search for identity, as all of these explorations help them figure out what they like or are good at doing and how they're unique. When most college-age people are asked, "What are you going *to do*?" many will simply respond with something like, "I'm not sure; I'm still trying to figure out what I want." This statement is proof that they're still in the process of forming an identity.

> Our role as spiritual leaders is to help people answer these questions through the lens of faith—and give them a safe place to do it.

Let me explain by using my daughter Hope as an illustration. Hope is two years old, and she clearly has very limited explorations in life. This, coupled with her youth and a lack of abstract thinking capabilities, obviously leaves her with an extremely limited sense of who she is as a person. But as she gets older, she'll be exposed to a lot more things and will eventually be able to think more abstractly. She'll begin to separate her identity from our family and gain a sense of who she is independently. This process of becoming self-aware is a very normal, healthy, and necessary process. It can be more complex and frustrating for some than others, but it's something everyone goes through. It's the way we move from being a dependent child to an independent adult.

The process may be frustrating, but it's not the core problem. The real problem exists in the fact that far too many college-age people are going through this process outside of loving faith communities. I believe it's part of the body of Christ's role to walk with college-age people through that space between. This is where your ministry comes in.

Let's go back to Nick for a second. It was his identity in Christ and his sense of belonging in the body of Christ that gave him perspective and even a role at his workplace. Because his identity is embraced in his faith—not in what he *does for a living*—his purpose at work is far beyond going through the motions and getting a paycheck or promotion. If he'd separated his identity from Christ and the church, it's likely that he would have made a very different decision and taken that other job.

So my point is simply that all these relationships work together. Our role is to help college-age people think through their identities (beginning with their beliefs), make sure they're connected in the body of Christ, and help them live out who they are in the world. It was so encouraging to talk to Nick and see how his faith was navigating his life. In his words, he'd be lost without his sense of belonging in the church—the body of Christ. It gives him a role and a sense of belonging in the world. All three relationships are intertwined.

PUZZLE PIECES

It's our job as spiritual leaders to guide this process and give college-age people a sense of belonging in our churches. And, just to be clear, I intentionally didn't say "our ministries." It's the church as a whole. Without this, people are left aimless in the world.

Your ministry to college-age people, individually, can help them put all the pieces of the puzzle together. What this requires of you is your time. You can put together a great message or small-group study on this idea, but more is needed. You need to individually walk people through this process and then help other older believers do the same. Give your college-age people a place to belong—one at a time.

THE BOTTOM LINE

- College-age people want to belong in the church as a whole, not just a ministry.

- To gain a sense of belonging, people look to three relationships: With themselves, with God, and with others in the world.

- These three relationships are intertwined. Helping people embrace their identities in Christ and find belonging in the body of Christ is what ultimately gives them a sense of belonging in the world.

- Helping someone through this process takes a lot of time—but it's worth it.

NOTES:

SECTION TWO

A Pra
Susta

Addressing the Unique
Needs of Your Ministry

CHAPTER 7

RECRUITING OLDER ADULTS—OVERCOMING OBSTACLES

I was recently setting up for a conference seminar when a middle-aged man approached me with a question. He said, "I was recently asked to be a part of the college ministry in my church, but I don't necessarily consider myself a good teacher or strong leader. So I was wondering if this seminar would be a help to me." In other words, because he wasn't a teacher or strong leader, he was questioning whether or not he could even have a role in the life of a college-age person. I told him we were going to be looking at what college-age people need from older believers and this seminar would be perfect for him.

At the end of the seminar, he came up to me again and told me he was glad he'd attended and that he really felt confident in his role. That was exactly what I wanted to hear and I tried to encourage him. He seemed like such a cool guy, had a great heart, and just wanted to invest in college-age people. It's people like him who need to be involved in our ministries. But when we think of leaders we mostly think of Type A people who are comfortable in front of people, can teach in large(r) formats, and are able to convince others to be involved. This initial thought certainly isn't wrong, but we can't stop with this definition of a leader. For our conversation, it's not even where we start.

We must consider a new breed of leader when we think about ministry to college-age people. When we need leaders for our junior high ministry, we look for characteristics in people that fit the uniqueness of that ministry. Yet the same is true with ministry to college-age people. Finding the right kind of leaders for your ministry is probably going to be an important part of your role. But if you're anything like me, there are a few obstacles you have to overcome before people jump on board.

The approach to ministry that I've proposed in this book forces a few battles to be fought. So I want to address three major obstacles that you may be facing in recruiting older volunteers:

1. Convincing the two generations that they have something in common

2. Helping the older generation overcome their feelings of intimidation around the younger generation

3. Helping the younger generation understand that the older generation has something unique to offer them

I want to address these issues now, and then in the next chapter we'll look at some *very* specific characteristics in the leaders we need.

SENSE OF ONENESS—FINDING COMMON GROUND

As I stated in chapter 6, college-age people desire to be a part of a church, not just a ministry. A specific ministry can be a starting point, but there's eventually a craving for more. So overcoming the sense of a lack of commonality between the two generations is crucial. And starting in the right direction requires the right kind of people.

We need leaders who are already relationally connected to different types of people. They may have friends who are in different generations. Maybe they know a single mom, parents of preschoolers, and empty nesters. These don't have to be intimate, lifelong friendships. The key is that they're relationally connected to different types of people in the church. It's these people being involved in the beginning of our ministry that will naturally bridge college-age people to the larger body.

It might seem as though we're looking for social butterflies, but that's not necessarily true. There's a middle-aged couple in my church, Mark and Kathleen,[13] who happen to be very introverted. It takes effort on their parts to initiate a

> We need leaders who are already relationally connected to different types of people. It's these people being involved in the beginning of our ministry that will naturally bridge college-age people to the larger body.

13. Their names have been changed to protect their privacy.

conversation, much less an intimate relationship with someone. But even though they don't walk into a room looking for someone to greet, if you get them with a person one-on-one—no matter what that person's life- or age-stage may be—they can connect. Over the past couple of years, Mark and Kathleen have become very connected to different types of people in our church. And this is exactly the type of people we want to start with in our ministries.

I have to play a role in getting leaders like Mark and Kathleen involved relationally with college-age people, and you may need to do the same. I started by simply getting to know them. My wife and I went on a date night with them, and I got together with Mark for lunches and an occasional early morning cup of coffee. I enjoy spending time with Mark, but there's something happening beyond my relationship with him. You see, I'm also modeling what I'd love for him to do with a college-age person. We're getting to know one another. I'm disclosing myself to him and vice versa. We're developing a relationship. These are exactly the same things I want Mark to do with a college-age guy. Put yet another way, in order to be the bridge of relationships, we have to first be in them.

Our Relationships Will Be the Bridge for Others

At the same time that I was getting to know Mark and Kathleen, I was also spending time with a college-age guy named Billy.[14] I'd meet with him every other week or so, and we'd talk through all kinds of issues. Like Mark, Billy is an introverted person. So based on personality alone, he probably never would have connected with a guy like Mark without someone else being involved.

I noticed an area of commonality between Billy and Mark—vocational interest. And then I simply talked to Billy about my friend Mark who was in that career and shared why I thought it would be good for Billy to connect with Mark. I also talked to Mark about how a young guy named Billy was interested in his career path.

I eventually asked Mark if he'd be willing to chat with Billy and answer any questions he might have about Mark's career. Mark agreed, so I asked Billy if he'd be open to hanging out with Mark for a cup of coffee sometime to *talk shop* for a bit. Billy agreed, too. So I went ahead and made the connection by letting Billy know that Mark would be calling him to set up

---

14. His name has been changed to protect his privacy.

a time to meet. (I've found it's best to have the older adult call the younger one.) Both men knew me, so I was able to be the bridge for this new relationship. It wasn't forced or formal, it was just a connection.

It's important to see the bigger picture in order to make these simple connections. Over time the obstacle of generational chasms has been overcome in both Mark and Billy's lives. Billy now knows some of Mark and Kathleen's friends, and he often hangs out with them. Plus, Mark and Kathleen have gotten to know some of Billy's friends. This takes time, of course, but leaders like Mark and Kathleen will individually and naturally bridge college-age people to the church body as a whole. The more Billy gets to know Mark and Kathleen, the more he'll be exposed to other aspects of their life. And this creates a sense of oneness and belonging to the life of the church that people his age long for.

Churches with leaders who help connect people will end up with generations that feel the commonality and a culture of oneness that's attractive for college-age people. It starts one person at a time. Remember, you don't have to change the culture overnight. You just have to start somewhere—like investing in one college-age person. Whatever the case, over time you can help others get connected in the same way.

OVERCOMING INTIMIDATION

Older believers typically face a few challenges when they think about investing in college-age people. For example many don't know what to do or say when they meet with someone. This can cause them (or you) to wonder if they have anything to offer. At the core of this uncertainty are feelings of intimidation and insecurity, which hinder them from initiating these relationships. So helping people overcome this obstacle is a vital part of our ministry.

Sometimes when we ask people to help in the college ministry, they get overwhelmed because they imagine having to lead something formal. They often feel as though they need a book to go through, a curriculum to follow, or some sort of Bible study to lead when they meet with a college-age person. It can be very intimidating for some older adults, especially those who don't consider themselves to be teachers or leaders. And although these types of resources can be useful, it's important to realize they aren't necessary.

The most helpful thing I've found to build confidence in older believers is emphasizing the need for their experience. Their role is simple: Allow God to use what he's already done in their lives in the life of another. I ask our adults to be an ear, a shoulder, and—when their life experiences can help someone—a mouthpiece.

When older adults realize others need their wisdom gained through life experience, two very important things happen. First, they aren't as intimidated because they have more wisdom than younger people do. Oftentimes the college-age person knows more about Scripture, but they don't have the wisdom of embracing what they know. This is where the older believer can help. Second, when they realize it's their experience that's needed, they tend to relax. They're not trying to teach a lesson, they're just being themselves. And this is when a genuine relationship can begin.

Our role is helping leaders catch the simplicity of investing in one person by using what they've already learned through life experience. That's it. Of course, if you have a spiritually maturing leader, then it's likely that over time their conversations with a college-age person will naturally include biblical truth. But it's through conversation and relationship that this occurs. If a formality develops naturally over time, that's fine; but it shouldn't start there. It starts with relational connection.

Having a relational focus not only allows older believers to impart godly wisdom based on life experience (versus just information), but also helps college-age people feel connected to the *lives* of people—which is exactly what we're trying to do. Through this connection they begin to feel a part of *the whole* of the church. Leaders don't need to feel as though they must reach an entire generation. We just need to encourage them to share their lives with one person—one day at a time.

Once we make the connection as leaders, we can then step back and pray for a natural mentor relationship to develop. If that doesn't happen, then at least the college-age person was exposed to an older adult. It's a starting point, and we can look for other opportunities for connection—for both the older and younger person.

> When older adults realize others need their wisdom gained through life experience, they aren't as intimidated and they relax.

HELPING YOUNGER GENERATIONS

On the other side of the fence, there can be college-age people who don't necessarily see the value in having someone invest in them. There can be a whole slew of reasons for this, but there is hope regardless of what those might be. First off, the way we phrase the importance of having a connection to an older believer is important. Initially, it might be unappealing if we talk about how college-age people should be "mentored" by someone. This can come across as very cold and formal. So rather than trying to create a formal mentorship program, it's helpful to take advantage of life's circumstances in a more natural way.

When Sarah's[15] mom died, it was a devastating and unforeseen loss for her. At 19, her world was abruptly turned upside down. A couple of weeks after the funeral, I asked Sarah how she was holding up. She said she was doing okay, but she was obviously missing her mom. She shared with me some guilty feelings she was having and wondered if she'd ever get past them. She also brought up how she had some real regrets—how she wished she could have just one more conversation with her mom. As she talked, I kept thinking of Maria,[16] a 35-year-old lady who'd just lost her mom about six months earlier. I talked to Sarah about Maria and shared with her that it might be good to sit down with someone who'd been through a similar situation. I told Sarah a little bit about why I thought it could be good for the two of them to talk. She agreed, so I made the connection.

Up to this point Sarah wasn't open to meeting with anyone older. But her circumstances had brought her to a point where she could see the value of talking with someone who was further along in life than she was. I brought to her attention someone who'd walked this path prior to her and who had some experience living through it. I knew she could really benefit from a relationship with Maria, and the circumstance provided a natural connecting point.

This is pretty much the same thing I did with Billy and Mark. Billy was thinking through different career paths, and it just so happened that he was interested in Mark's vocation. Because I knew both of them, I could capitalize on the natural life circumstances.

There can certainly be more than one person in the ministry or church who is working to bridge relationships like this. (Give it a little time, and it will

---

15. Her name has been changed to protect her privacy.
16. Her name has been changed to protect her privacy.

happen naturally.) But regardless of the number, our focus must be on one relationship at a time.

It's also important to note that trials and vocation aren't the only natural points of connection. There are always points in time when college-age idealism and life theory don't work out as we thought. It's like young couples who have all kinds of theories on parenting—until they have a child. Then their theories go out the window, and they're much more open to receiving input from other parents.

This scenario happens to all of us at one point or another, and these are precisely the times we want to capitalize on in our ministries. College-age people have questions about relationships and marriage. They have friendships that fall apart, parents who get divorced, loved ones who die, times of confusion regarding sexuality or their beliefs, and of course the longing for life direction that's often so hard to grasp. These are the times when I've seen them be very open to having an outside voice speak into their lives. We just need to be there to see the need and make the connections.

I understand there can be things like personality differences or even specific quirks that can be turn-offs and hinder an ongoing relationship between two people. This is precisely why we should be very specific about the people we ask to be involved. We need people who have some very specific characteristics, which I'll talk through in next chapter.

THE BOTTOM LINE

- Finding commonality between people in different generations and then personally connecting them based on that sameness is vital for helping the generations come together.

- We need to help older adults understand the need for and the role of their life experience. When we do, they'll overcome the intimidation they feel about investing in younger people.

- Being aware of the challenges that college-age people face can greatly assist us in showing them their need to have more experienced people in their lives.

NOTES:

CHAPTER 8

RECRUITING OLDER ADULTS— CHARACTERISTICS TO LOOK FOR

A guy in my church once made an appointment to let me know that he wanted to *disciple* a college-age person. Typically these are times of encouragement. I get excited whenever someone wants to invest his or her time and talents in this way. But as I talked with him, it was obvious that he was in no place to do so. He was struggling with a few different sin issues, he was incredibly legalistic, and he just kept talking and talking—not listening to me at all.

I don't mean to sound harsh, but the truth is that some older believers will only repel a college-age person. It's just a fact of life. Therefore we need to be careful of this—even to the point of not allowing certain adults to be involved. I know it's tough to say no to someone—especially when we're desperate for more volunteers. But we need to have the right people involved. If not, then the involvement of the wrong people could be more damaging than having nobody involved at all.

We need to be very intentional about the adults we ask to get involved. You might already have an idea of who would be good and who wouldn't. But I want to make this as practical as possible by listing some specific characteristics that I've seen work well with college-age people.

I want to preface this list by making it clear that the people we're looking for defy economic categories. It doesn't matter if they're business owners or stay-at-home moms, introverts or extroverts, single or married, musicians or engineers, loaded or broke—the more variety, the better. Not only does a wide array of people increase the chances that our college-age people will find someone with whom to connect, but it also reinforces the idea that what you do and what you have doesn't define who you are. These are very important issues to keep in mind. We want to make sure we place a healthy value on the differences in people, so we need to make sure the adults investing in our college-age people defy categories.

WHAT TO LOOK FOR

There are some specific characteristics I've found to be most beneficial in older adults who work with college-age people. Not every adult will have all of these, but let these characteristics serve as a mental checklist during your search.

> Characteristics to look for in older adults to work with college-age people include: Relaxed, older, ask good questions, learners, biblically sound, solid marriage, encouragers, a heart for people, connected to the life of the church, vulnerable.

Relaxed

Since our goal is to bridge relational connections, we're looking for people who are relaxed and have no agenda other than getting to know someone and allowing someone to get to know them. We need to set the vision for our leaders that they're simply letting the God-given experiences in their lives be used in the life of another. Through conversation and getting to know each other, their experience will speak for itself. There doesn't need to be an agenda going into these meetings. Even those with the best intentions can have a detrimental effect on the group if they act as though they're going to *fix* the college-age people, or if they're easily frustrated by the young adults' inconsistency and lack of discipline. The ideal volunteers are those who are willing to be patient with younger people and won't freak out and feel like they need to immediately solve every little issue in a person's life.

Older

College-age people desire to be connected to someone older, but there are some variations and circumstances that can dictate who we connect them to. For instance, if they're interested in a particular vocation, it could be good to connect them with someone who's just a few years into that career, versus someone who's about to retire. It doesn't have to be this way, as you saw with Mark and Billy; but sometimes connecting them with someone who's still getting a feel for what it's like to start off on a particular career path is good.

Again, the category the person falls under isn't important. It's simply a matter of connecting a college-age person with someone who's involved in the church, who shares something in common with the younger person that makes the connection more natural, and who is older.

We can be intentional in other areas as well. For example if the college-age person's parents are divorced and he or she grew up in a single-parent home, then connecting him or her with a married person who's around the same age as the divorced parents can be beneficial. This older person might fill a parental role that the college-age person longs for.

Another idea is to begin by asking the college-age person what type of person he or she would like to meet with. This is a great place to start, and since you're already connected to a variety of people anyway, you can likely find someone who could be a match.

Ask Good Questions

The older people we seek will be more interested in finding information than giving it. They'll ask questions about family history, desires, pursuits, and relationships because they want to get to know the person they're meeting with. And ideally, they'll ask questions that help college-age people think through things in a way that will lead them toward biblically mature conclusions. (See chapter 10 for some examples of questions they can ask.)

An example of a good question is something that gets the younger person thinking more deeply about whatever the issue is. Ask college-age people a "what" question, and they can probably give a decent answer. But ask them a "why" question, and you'll see them squirm a bit. Good questions get down to the "why" of the answers. This exchange creates a natural dialogue and gives both parties the chance to get to know each other on a much more intimate level.

Learners

One of the greatest attributes to have is honesty and a willingness to dialogue about issues. We want people who will ask for the thoughts of college-age people for their own lives and seek their perspective about their families or churches. When college-age people observe older adults being teachable, they'll follow. On the other hand, a know-it-all will repel college-age people. Therefore, our volunteers must be good listeners. When they ask a question, we want them to listen. They can't be the type of people who ask a question but don't listen to the answer because they immediately begin thinking about the next question they want to ask. Yeah, we need to be careful of this type of person.

Biblically Sound

We aren't necessarily looking for seminary-trained people, but we need people who are familiar enough with Scripture that they can guide people toward and through it. They need to be seeking to live by it and be mature enough to say, "I don't know" if they're asked a question they have no clue how to answer. Their maturity and humility allows them to come alongside younger people and learn *with* them—maybe even be taught by them at times. But they need to have a heart for Scripture and seek to live by it.

Have a Solid Marriage

This in no way negates the contributions of the younger single person or the older widow. I've just found this characteristic to be helpful, especially when more than half of college-age people have divorced parents and few, if any, Christ-centered marriages to look to. Generally speaking, college-age people have a desire to get married at some point in their lives, and they're figuring out how to achieve balance in their relationships. Therefore, they're interested in how different marriages work. Couples who are willing to be open about the strengths and weaknesses in their marriage are very appealing to college-age people. Volunteers who have a solid, godly marriage can be excellent examples for college-age people who are in the midst of developing their sense of identity and their understanding of what intimacy *really* looks like.

Natural Encouragers

You know how you can spend time with someone and just feel better afterward? That's a great characteristic to look for in an older volunteer. It can be someone who builds up others through words of encouragement, or a woman in your church who acts like a mom to anyone she runs into. Encouragers are important because as college-age people are getting to know themselves more deeply, they're also coming face-to-face with characteristics they don't like about themselves. This can be fairly difficult for some to process. But spending an hour with an older believer who really encourages them in life can be extremely beneficial.

Have a Heart for People, Not Their Accomplishments

The people we want serving college-age people should be solely interested in investing in the Individual as a human being. And they should be concerned about the character of the person *right now*, not what may eventually be. A lot of college-age people don't have a vocational direction, won't lead the largest church in North America, and won't be a CEO. But all of them are worth the investment of our time and talents, and they can have a huge impact on and in the body of Christ.

College-age people are truly in between in a lot of areas of their lives, and the future is usually unclear in every one of them. The rest of the world is putting pressure on them to *become* something other than who they currently are, and it's our volunteers who can walk alongside them and love them for who they are today. This, my friends, will go a very long way. The more love that college-age people feel today, the more confidence they'll have to move into tomorrow. Most college-age people aren't trying to be indecisive in their life direction; they just need to be encouraged instead of pressured.

Connected to the Life of the Church

The leaders we're looking for don't just attend a church service, a small group, or a Sunday school class. They have relationships with different types of people—particularly outside of any formal gathering like the ones I just mentioned. Of course some may be more connected than others, but this is an important characteristic for accomplishing our goal of connecting college-age people to the body as a whole. One of the mistakes we can make is assuming we've done our job by just connecting college-age people to one adult. This is why I've purposely stated our goal as connecting them to the life of the church, which implies more than one person or family. Sure, we start one person at a time. But having volunteers who are already connected provides a natural bridge to others in the church as well.

Vulnerable

Those who are willing to be vulnerable about sharing their weaknesses and struggles are going to attract college-age people. College-age people are easily repelled by leaders who try to be perfect. They're fully aware that it's only a façade. So having volunteers who are willing to be open about their own dysfunction will be an important characteristic to look for.

They Are Who They Are

We don't need people who feel the need to be cool. I was speaking at a high school camp and got to know a youth pastor named Joe.[17] He's been in youth ministry for more than 30 years, and I saw him hanging out with kids all weekend. He wasn't trying to be anything other than himself, and I believe this is why kids were attracted to him. He has a goofy side to his personality that the kids see, but it's just a part of who he is. People know if we're authentic—and it could be argued that college-age people are more in tune with this attribute than anyone else. We need to make sure our volunteers are comfortable with who they are and are willing to allow younger people to get to know them.

Authentic Faith

Older volunteers are role models for what I hope to see develop in our college-age people. So I want them to be people who don't just profess the faith but seek to have their faith shape every aspect of their lives.

Dependable

The volunteers we're looking for have a consistency about them. They're where they say they'll be, they're on time, and they always follow through and follow up with people. This characteristic is critical when working with college-age people who are generally not many of these things. Thus, having people model these positive characteristics for them is an important part of our ministry.

---

17. His name has been changed to protect his privacy.

Understand the Difference Between Belonging and Acceptance

People have a sense of belonging when they're loved as they are. Acceptance implies there's still a long way to go before a person will actually fit in. Our volunteers have to give college-age people the sense of belonging they long for. It doesn't mean they can't issue challenges or push people toward maturity, but it does require them to walk with people no matter what they initially do with the challenges. Again, college-age people want to feel like they belong in the body versus just being accepted.

A Couple More Thoughts

I realize this list is rather daunting—especially when you're desperate to find any volunteers, much less those who meet all of these expectations. But I want to encourage you that there are people in your church who exhibit some of these characteristics. They don't have to master every area to be effective. They just need to be people who exhibit some of these attributes and are working toward the rest of them in their own lives. They might not stand out as the cool people or the obvious choices to work with college-age people. But I promise you that adults who have the potential to be effective in bringing college-age people toward Christlikeness are in your church.

Also, college-age people crave help with seeking a direction in life, and they have all kinds of questions they'd like to ask older adults. But just know that they also want the space and freedom to figure things out for themselves. They want to have someone to talk to, but not all the time. They don't mind having a mentor, but they don't want another parent. We want adults who will pursue a relationship with a college-age person, but having them around too much can actually be detrimental.

The amount of time they spend with someone through our ministry depends on the person, but this has to be watched. We don't want to smother people; we want to make sure these connections are natural and relational. And I've found the best way to go about this is by starting with your friends. If you develop a *staff* of older adults, it can create an awkwardness in your ministry. And if you're not careful, these friends can feel like chaperones.

> Volunteers don't have to master every area to be effective. They just need to be people who exhibit some of these attributes and are working toward the rest of them in their own lives.

No college-age person wants a chaperone.

I've found it beneficial to think of your older adult volunteers as waiting in the wings. The majority of the adults involved in our ministry have never attended one of our weekly gatherings. They were people whom I got to know and love, so I asked them if they'd be willing to walk alongside our younger people in the context of life—not a program in our church. I'd encourage you to make that distinction with those whom you ask to volunteer as well. You're not asking them to commit to a program; they're committing to one person.

THE BOTTOM LINE

- The adult leaders we seek defy economic categories or vocational paths, but we want to look for those with specific personal characteristics.

- Older adults can't look at college-age people as problems that need to be immediately fixed. They need to be in it for the long-term relationship.

- College-age people don't want another parent or chaperone. They just need someone to talk to every once in a while about what's going on in their lives.

NOTES:

CHAPTER 9
LEADING COLLEGE-AGE LEADERS

One of the first words that comes to mind when I think about college-age people is *potential*. In my mind there isn't a better word in the English language to describe them. They are zealous, they have the freedom and passion to do whatever they want, they want to make an impact on the world, and many are seeking to do so in some way. They clearly want to be a part of something bigger than themselves. Give them a chance to lead the charge in something, and they will. Give them freedom in leadership, and they can take your ministry to levels you couldn't have reached yourself. Allow them to make decisions, and you'll be surprised at how well some of them process through the issues.

At the same time, I could have easily restated all of the above from a different perspective: "Give them a chance to lead the charge in something, and you'll see them make some major mistakes. Give them freedom in leadership, and they'll drop the ball. Allow them to make decisions, and you'll have to clean up a ton of messes."

Both sides are true.

Allowing college-age people to lead will force you to deal with both sides, but that's part of the beauty of this ministry. We can sit back and watch God use them and use *us* in their development.

We ought to allow them to lead, assume responsibility, and—to some degree— tell us what should be done in our ministries. But that doesn't mean we don't have to lead them, nor does it excuse our responsibility to maintain some balance.

TIPS FOR LEADING LEADERS

Over the past 12 years, I've realized there are 11 things that are really important to keep in mind with peer leaders in a college ministry.

1. Start With Those Who Are Connected

This is one area of life where I'm okay with the top-down theory. If you want the people in your ministry to be connected to the life of your church, then every one of the leaders has to be first. It doesn't make sense otherwise. Part of organizing your ministry toward a goal (connection to the body of Christ) is making sure that all of the pieces feed into that particular area. And so starting with college-age people who are connected to older adults in your church isn't just good—it's necessary. This sets the pace for your ministry and will help provide sustainability for it.

2. Be Slow to Put People in Leadership

One of the best lessons I learned through the years is to take things slowly. And this is especially true when it comes to putting people into leadership positions. One area we need to be very careful of is balancing how we develop giftedness and character. College-age people aren't lacking in giftedness, but character can be an issue. Now, I know plenty of college-age people who have a very solid character, but I also know those who have giftedness that far surpasses their character.

By way of confession I'll admit that this was my story when I was younger. I had some teaching and leadership gifts, but my character was way behind. I wasn't living a crazy lifestyle by any means; but then again I didn't have to be walking on the wild side for my character to be lacking.

It's said that giftedness gets you places, but it's your character that keeps you there. We need to focus on the character of people and intentionally think through whether or not giving them a leadership position (in any capacity) is best for their long-term character development.

We don't usually think about it this way. We see someone's gifts and typically focus on helping that person develop those gifts by releasing him or her into ministry. But oftentimes this can lead to a damaged heart and potentially one that's filled with so much pride that it hinders the longevity of the person's ministry. So I'd encourage you to be very mindful of who you place in leadership. They don't need to be perfect (we certainly aren't), but there ought to be a balance between how we lead them in developing their character and utilizing their giftedness.

A tension in all of this is that college-age people have a tendency to push for their gifts to be developed and may feel as though they're being unfaithful if they're unable to use their gifts. I've even had some people feel stifled when their gifts weren't being used as much as *they* thought was appropriate. This dissatisfaction usually isn't caused by ill motives as much as it is by ignorance and a lack of wisdom. They want to be used by God, which is a great thing! But they have limited life experience to help them see what God *really* wants for them. He desires them to be Christlike in character, not necessarily to be used like Christ was used. Differentiating this for them can be a very lengthy process, but it's worth it.

I've had many interns over the years, and I've had to hold back some of them from doing certain things. I didn't hold them back because they couldn't do the job; I did it because I thought it could hinder their character development. Truthfully some didn't like this at all and felt like I was hindering them from ministry. But there have also been those who humbly took the counsel, worked on their character, and continued being teachable.

> I'm all for helping someone develop their gifts, but I'm much more interested in helping people develop Christlike character.

I'm all for helping someone develop their gifts, and I believe it's a part of my role to do so. But I'm much more interested in helping people develop Christlike character. It's great to see college-age people being used by God. But if their character won't sustain them, then I don't mind being the bad guy.

These decisions aren't easy ones to make, but my focus is on how I can invest in people as Christ followers, not what they can do for our ministry. That's why I suggest taking it slowly. When we do what's best for the individual, we *are* doing what's best for the ministry.

3. Truly Love People

If you open your Bible to 1 Corinthians chapter 13, you'll see a description of love. I think it's interesting that the first word used to describe love is *patience*. It implies a long-term mindset and insinuates that we aren't looking for immediate results as much as we desire the long-term health of someone. This certainly ties into my previous point regarding the importance of investing in the character of individuals more than their giftedness. But it also leads us to a new point that says we need to allow them to not be perfect and we need to be okay with that. People require time to develop. All of us are in process. Just because we may be further along in certain areas, that doesn't make us better. In fact I'm around college-age people who seem to be further along than I am in some areas.

When college-age people lead, they will fail, make really dumb decisions, jeopardize certain things, and even hurt people. So our patience is necessary. We need to walk alongside them and guide them with love, patiently and gently. The point is not to keep them from failing; it's to help them learn after they do fail. And that takes patience.

4. Give Freedom

As the leader of the ministry, you probably have ideas and a way of doing things that work well for you. We all do and we should to some degree. But one of the things I've found is that allowing college-age people to have the freedom to do it their own way often works out better than I could have done it.

I remember brainstorming with a team for one of our mission trips to Romania. We were putting on a camp for orphans, so we were thinking about games to do with the kids. I threw out some initial ideas, and some students took it from there. As they were working through how to do things, I quickly realized it was going to be much better than I could have ever dreamed. They not only had better ideas, but because they had freedom, they also thought through how to implement them. The truth is that college-age people, when they're given freedom, can blow us away with their creativity, thoughtfulness, and even implementation. Step in when needed, but give your leaders freedom. Be patient and allow them to work through problems on their own. If you're anything like me, you may discover that your idea wasn't so good after all.

5. Trust Them

Actually trusting college-age people goes further than we realize. They want to know that their ideas and input are taken seriously. They want to take on something and show us they can complete it. Of course, sometimes they'll flake out on us and leave major things undone. We just have to use those times as opportunities to help them grow, not excuses to withhold our trust. You might be surprised at how much trust from one's spiritual leaders means to people. Working with college-age leaders is more about releasing them with trust and then guiding their failures than it is about making sure people prove themselves before we offer our trust.

6. Ask Tough Questions

College-age people are becoming acutely aware of not only their own gifts, but also the gifts of others. This mindfulness is a great help in becoming self-aware, but it can also cause them to feel defeated when they see that other people are as good—or better—at doing something as they are. I've seen many college-age people pursue leadership roles out of pride or envy, rather than a true desire to serve. I've also seen them fall into a kind of false humility—the kind they often learn from growing up in the church—that helps them avoid taking responsibility for their weaknesses and failures. The results are never healthy for them or the ministry.

This is why we have to personally spend time with them and ask some of the tough questions about pride and envy. We can ask *what* they want to do, but asking *why* they want to do it is better. I've found that asking college-age people very direct questions is best. We have to be careful of the all-too-frequent "Sunday school answers" they might give us and make sure they're in tune with both their pure and *impure* motivations. Helping them in this area brings about self-awareness as well as character development.

I ask very blunt questions such as, "When you're not playing guitar and Tim is, do you get jealous?" Or "Was it hard for you to not be in charge of that event?" And sometimes I'll even be more direct by asking something like, "Was it hard to sit back and watch Suzy take all of that on and not come to you for help?" After we talk about questions like this, I always ask *why* they felt the way they did.

I'm not suggesting that you should assume they're jealous or envious of others, but it never hurts to ask the tough questions. If nothing else, it lets them know you're more concerned about their character than what they might be able to do in the ministry.

7. Recognize Idealism

For me, one of the most enjoyable aspects of working with college-age people is their idealism. They can dream, they have the ideal in mind, and they want to work toward that. Sometimes there can be a loss of reality with this mindset; but nevertheless, it's a lot of fun to be around. Plus it pushes me. As we get older we can lose our sense of idealism, and we need to be prodded a bit in this area.

Yet at the same time, the downside to idealism is arrogance. College-age people think through a lot of things, in theory, but they have limited experience in living out those concepts. I have a formula for this: Knowledge minus life experience equals arrogance. (Knowledge - Life Experience = Arrogance) One way that we can know this formula applies to someone is that the person will tend to criticize every other model or approach that doesn't match how he or she has thought through it.

We see this in theology, too. Hang around a Bible college or seminary theology class for a while. They're thinking through the information and intellectualizing the implications, but they don't necessarily live them out. And because they're still in a theoretical and ideal world, they tend to be arrogant. This is where our patience comes in. College-age people are thinking and intellectualizing everything from relationships to morality. But their life experience is lacking in living out those theories—at least for the most part.

Time eventually takes care of this. We can try telling college-age people differently, and at times that might be appropriate. But they really just need to go through life a bit more. As they're gaining more experience, they will inevitably discover that their theories don't always work out the way they'd thought. This is when knowledge begins turning into wisdom and when our patience really pays off. Just recognize idealism when it's present, sit back, and patiently pray for them to grow in godly wisdom.

8. Guide Undisciplined Areas

College-age people typically struggle with discipline and organization—remember that feeling? Working with college-age volunteer leaders will often test our patience, but our role is to give them the right combination of guidance and freedom. I shoot for a kind of relaxed formality where I'm clear about what I expect from them but gracious when they forget a detail or lose focus. Having a personal relationship with them can make all the difference in these circumstances. The more we know someone on an intimate level, the more we get to know their weaknesses—and they learn about ours as well. I find that most college-age people already know they have a hard time with discipline, and they're usually eager for help in this area. So when a detail slips or they don't follow through on a commitment, we can talk about it as a life issue, not a ministry problem. And differentiating these two things with your college-age leaders is a very important thing to keep in mind. Address the character and life issue, not the impact it had on the ministry.

9. Be Careful of Dating Relationships

Lots of dating relationships start and end in college ministry. They can add strength and joy, or they can add drama and destruction—especially when one or both of the people involved are in leadership. Because college-age people are socially motivated, these types of situations can cause major tension in groups of friends and can even have a ripple effect on the whole ministry. As leaders we need to keep an eye on dating relationships and intervene when we see problems—even potential problems.

One time a dating couple in our ministry planned to go on the same mission trip. In December, when we picked our teams for the July trip, they'd been dating for a few months, and everything was going well. So they thought it would be great to be on the same team. I wasn't so sure. So I moved one of them to a different team, one that would be serving two weeks earlier than the other one. The timing meant that between their two trips, they wouldn't see each other for a month.

They initially thought this was cruel of me to do, but a month after we purchased the plane tickets, they broke up. If they'd been on the same trip, it could have been a major disruption for the rest of the team. And even if they'd stayed together, the time apart could have been very beneficial for their relationship anyway. It was an unpopular decision on my part, but I believe it was in everyone's best interest. These decisions aren't fun to make, nor are they popular. And we want to be careful not to unnecessarily interfere. However, sometimes stepping in and erring on the side of caution is best.

I've had other situations where a dating relationship affected the ministry as well. For instance a worship leader dates someone in the group and then breaks her heart. You can't stop this from happening, but the truth is that these types of things can have a lasting impact. Once the couple breaks up, an entire group of friends could leave the ministry. College-age people are excited to leave the high school relational drama, but they don't realize that the drama often continues. We don't want to hinder a relationship, but protecting the people and the ministry is a line you may need to walk. Some breakups will cause more waves than others, and we don't want it to affect our decision making too much. But being aware of potential tension within dating relationships is important—especially when the people involved are in leadership.

10. Protect Identity Substitution

Some people, like those who've grown up in the church, can have an identity based solely in a ministry role. As leaders we can all struggle with this at some level, but we really need to be sensitive of this with college-age leaders. They're still in the process of developing a sense of identity, and even though we want them to discover that in the context of the body of Christ, finding it in a ministry leadership role isn't necessarily what we want for them.

This is really important to keep in mind with newer believers. When someone comes to a saving knowledge of Christ, they often want to get involved immediately. And we typically allow them to do so. Although this could be beneficial, it can also be dangerous. So keeping a balance is necessary. I've seen so many people move forward in a role without ever experiencing what it means to just be a part of the body of Christ.

Samuel[18] is a great example. About three months after he became a Christian, our worship leader asked him to play in the band. Before we knew it, he was filling in and leading worship. Then, three years down the road, Samuel sat in my office one day and said he needed to step down because he'd never "not been in leadership." He felt the need to "just be a part of the church." I remember that day vividly, and that conversation completely changed my

---

18. His name has been changed to protect his privacy.

perspective on this issue. While it's not a hard-and-fast rule, giving a new believer 6 to 12 months before offering them a leadership role might be a good guideline. We don't want someone to cross the line by allowing his or her identity as a worship leader (or any other ministry position) to be a substitute for an identity as a child of God.

> We don't want someone to cross the line by allowing his or her identity as a worship leader (or any other ministry position) to be a substitute for an identity as a child of God.

11. Constantly Look for New Leaders

We tend to wait for leaders to rise up, rather than raising them up ourselves. However, most leadership positions in a college ministry have about a two-year turnover rate, so we need to continue raising up new leaders. A few people will be around longer, but many will have moved on and others will have moved in. Pay attention to the recent high school grads coming in to your ministry. They'll have fresh energy and enthusiasm for what you're doing. I'm not saying you should put them in leadership before they're ready. Instead, put effort into building a relationship with them where you can develop their character...and potentially their giftedness.

THE BOTTOM LINE

- College-age people can be some of the most passionate volunteers we have, but we still need to disciple them.

- We ought to focus on developing the character of the people more than the roles they can fill or the tasks they can complete.

- We want to make sure we're helping people find an identity in Christ, not a role in our ministry.

NOTES:

CHAPTER 10

ONE-ON-ONE CONVERSATIONS—QUESTIONS TO ASK

One of the most intimidating things about ministry can be initiating or even sitting down with a college-age person one-on-one. If you're used to these types of meetings, this chapter may serve as a review of ideas and possibly provide some more focus. But if you're not used to doing this, it will help answer the questions you're probably asking yourself, such as: *What do I do during these times? What do I say? What am I supposed to accomplish? Do I need a resource or book to go through?*

Spending time one-on-one with people is one of the most impacting things we can do. This is why I want to share a few things that have greatly helped me in this area of ministry. They're very simple ideas but crucial.

I remember when I first started our ministry and I began meeting with people. Because I was the leader, everyone thought I just wanted to talk about the ministry or my vision for it. But my intentions were quite opposite. I wanted to get to know them as human beings. I knew that putting together a meeting to get something from them would be a huge turn-off. Instead, I wanted to invest in these people and build a relationship with them. That's it. But knowing how to go about that was a learning process.

There was a point when I viewed my meetings with people as a semi-formal time where we were supposed to do "spiritual things," whatever that meant. Usually it meant having an in-depth Bible study or extended prayer time. But then I realized that relationships take time to build. At the core of any relationship is getting to know one another. This requires me to ask questions and the other person to disclose who he or she is—and vice versa. In other words relationships are built one day at a time; they're rarely formal or structured. Once I understood this, I began to relax knowing that there wasn't any pressure on me to do anything in particular. In fact I found that the fewer expectations I put on any one conversation, the more effective it was. No agenda. I simply needed to get to know the person and allow him or her to get to know me.

This is the type of connection that college-age people desire. And this is where discipleship naturally happens—through relationship. One of the biggest things I learned is that when you're the leader of a ministry, people naturally ask you questions about faith issues. So through our conversations things will naturally come up anyway. We don't have to force it. As much as I'd like to believe that my teaching has impacted people, the truth is that *God* has used the time I've spent with them one-on-one. This doesn't mean I'm super spiritual. It just means I'm normal.

> This is where discipleship naturally happens— through relationship.

We all have people in our lives who've left a mark on us in some positive way. And some of them don't even know they did it. They just spent time with us or said one thing that somehow stuck with us all of these years. It's just being around the person that impacted us. And deep down inside we'd all love to be that person for someone else.

Preparing a great talk or small group Bible study probably won't have the greatest impact on the people in our ministry. It's the time we spend giving them our undivided attention. It's being available, there in person, and willing to hear them out or walk alongside them through the pains and joys of life that has lasting impact.

SETTING THE TONE

Over the years I've learned, mostly the hard way, several tricks for making sure the right tone is set for a meeting with someone:

(1) Make the appointment yourself. If you're in a larger ministry, you might have an administrative assistant who takes care of your schedule. But scheduling times with students cannot be one of those things you delegate to someone else. That sets the wrong tone, especially with someone who wants to meet with you for the first time.

(2) Whenever possible set the meeting place off the church campus. Let the person you're meeting pick a coffee shop or other neutral place. If we meet in an office, it's really hard for people who don't know us well to relax and just be themselves. But in a coffee shop, especially one the person goes to

often, it's different. It's down-to-earth, not formal. These things help create a relaxed tone for a conversation.

(3) Turn off your cell phone before you meet. I used to pick up whenever someone called or check my text messages when they came in. But then I realized how this negatively affected my time with people. This communicated that I'm busy, had to fit them into my schedule, and they weren't a priority. To be honest, I used to like it when people saw how busy I was. But this was a sickness in me that hindered my time with people. It put the focus on me when it should have been on them. So now I turn my cell phone on silent. And if I'm expecting a call from my wife, for instance, I simply let the person know right from the start that she might be calling. But I'm very clear about that being the only call I'll pick up while we're together.

(4) Whenever possible, make sure to arrive early. Walk into the place where you're meeting, find a table, turn off your phone, and wait patiently. If you're working or returning an email, shut everything down as soon as the person shows up. Make sure the people you meet with know that when they arrive, you are there for them. Nothing else.

(5) Don't have an agenda. Some people will come to you with a heavy heart, and you'll need to be an ear and shoulder for them. Other times people will come totally scatterbrained after a busy day, and you'll need to bounce around in conversation with them. And then there are times when people will float in very relaxed and possibly still half-asleep. If we come into a meeting with a set agenda of some kind—possibly a curriculum or book to go through—then we can miss what's happening in their lives. And this isn't something we want to miss. These are the very things we want to observe. We want to be there—fully there—to talk through anything that's happening in their lives.

To set the right tone for meeting with someone:
1. Make the appointment yourself.
2. Choose a meeting place away from the church.
3. Turn off your cell phone.
4. Arrive early.
5. Don't have an agenda.

DISCIPLESHIP THROUGH QUESTIONS

Balancing my desire to invest in someone as a spiritual leader yet keep a very relaxed tone in my relationship with that person is a bit tricky. So I've found that asking questions is a great way to keep a balance. It's through questions that we can get to know people better, be a part of guiding their thoughts, and do so in very natural ways. And, as somewhat of a side note, it's important to make a distinction between guiding thoughts and giving them. We can teach a bunch of biblical conclusions, walk people through a resource that does that…or we can walk alongside them in life and help them discover things for themselves. I believe the results are more lasting when people come to their own conclusions. There are certainly times when we can be more direct, but as a general rule we should be guiding thoughts versus giving them—and especially so with college-age people.[19]

To do this I've found that asking some very basic, yet specific questions really helps us go deeper into discussion. So I want to walk you through seven practical questions you can ask that lead to deeper conversations about identity and faith. Determining when to ask these questions will depend on the person we're meeting with or the current circumstances. But generally speaking, we can ask these fairly early on in our relationships with people. Here are the questions and a little bit about why they're good to ask.

What Commitments Do You Want to Shape Your Life?

This question is good to ask for a number of reasons. First, it helps college-age people think through commitment. Each of the five stages of identity that I discuss in College Ministry 101 has a commitment aspect to it. Some never commit, some overcommit, while others commit without realizing the implications of that commitment. So asking this question gets the idea of commitment to the front of their minds and hopefully forces them to move from one stage to the next.

Second, this question gets down to what they desire. College-age people are trying to figure out what they want. Many people are asking them what they're going to do with their lives, but they don't move toward that until they figure out what they want. In other words, this question will help them with a thought process they're already in. It's helping them figure out what they want to be committed to.

Notice that I didn't say what they are committed to. Once they figure out what they want to be committed to, we can help them differentiate those things with what they are committed to already. Most likely they're currently

19. For more on this, see the "Teaching and Discipleship" chapter (Chapter 9) in College Ministry 101.

doing things that undermine the very things they want in life. And it's at this point of the conversation that discipleship really begins. Our desire is to get them to the point where they *want* their commitment to God to shape their lives. What we commit to today will shape our lives tomorrow. So the key is getting them to a point where they're aligning their commitments with what they desire. It might take a dozen meetings to discuss this question fully, but it's worth the time.

How Do You Know You're a Christian?

This is a bit of a loaded question, I admit. We often ask questions like, "How did you become a Christian?" or even "When or how did you get saved?" But it's different to ask a question worded this way. This is a great question to get people thinking theologically, and it can launch you into a very long, yet healthy and fun conversation. The goal of asking this is to help them gain a sense of confidence in their salvation. But beware: The opposite might happen first. And this is where it gets fun.

Most of the time their response will have something to do with a time they remember praying. Challenge this. Ask them something like, "So, you *know* you're a Christian because you prayed one time?" You'll likely witness some intellectual gymnastics at this point. They might flounder around a bit, struggling to find an answer. But this is healthy. Although it might get a bit uncomfortable for them, we're actually helping them toward being more confident in who they are in Christ.

Eventually we can guide them toward seeing the fruits of the Spirit in their lives (Galatians 5:22-23), the transformation that's taken place (Romans 12:2), their obedience to Christ (John 15:10), and even the love they have for other believers (1 John 5:1). But letting them discover these things for themselves by asking them questions is a great and natural way of helping them get there.

What's the Difference Between a Faith and a Conscience?

So many college-age people, especially those who've grown up in the church, have more of a religious conscience than they do a personal faith. This question can take some explaining on your part, so I'll help you out here. The bottom-line difference is that we're not saved through a conscience;

we're saved through our faith (Ephesians 2:8). Helping college-age people differentiate between these two things is very important.

A conscience is gained by receiving information. What we're taught shapes our conscience. So it's possible to do certain things—or not do them—simply because we grew up being taught that way. College-age people are at the point where they're reevaluating all of the assumptions they grew up with. They're trying to figure out what they personally believe, versus just assuming something to be true because their parents believe that way. Thus, this question is just another way of helping them think through what they're already processing. It gets to the core of what they believe, and it's a natural way for us to join in on that journey.

Who Are You?

This question gets to the core issue of college-age people: Identity. Identity is not an issue; it's *the* issue that college-age people are thinking through. This might seem like a simple question, but it's not. It's a great question because it forces people to think about who they believe they are, who they believe they're perceived to be, and possibly even who they want to be. Perhaps most importantly, this question gives us clues as to how much their faith factors into their sense of themselves.

For the most part it doesn't. Most will initially respond with personality traits, career pursuits, or likes and dislikes. The final stage of natural identity formation in college-age people, as mentioned previously, is what I call the *Theologian stage*. I'm not saying they need to be seminary-trained; I'm simply suggesting that their sense of identity is seen in who they've been made into through Christ. The theologian would answer this question by saying something like, "I'm a child of God." They not only verbalize this, but they seek to embrace it.

Now, embracing our identity solely in Christ is an ongoing process for all of us—one that's never fully embraced here on earth, unfortunately. But we want to help people get to the point where they desire to embrace this truth and are pursuing it. And we can make them aware of our continuing process in this area as well. It's a fun conversation to have with someone, for sure. But most importantly, we can learn how we might assist them in discovering their spiritual identity before anything else.

What Do Others Want from You?

The biggest reason I ask this question is that it allows me to see the pressures they're feeling from other people. The college-age years are filled with pressure, but every person experiences different challenges and handles them differently as well. This question might give us insight into their relationship with their parents, a boss, or even the pressure they put on themselves. It can lead the conversation in dozens of directions, but it helps them think through what's weighing on them and gives us insight into how we might be able to encourage them. Ultimately, of course, we can guide this conversation toward what God wants from them. And helping them focus here, possibly negating all other pressures, is the place we want them to get to.

What Do Others Want *for* You?

This question is a great follow-up to the previous one. For instance if they feel pressure *from* their parents, then this question might help them see past the pressure and into their parents' motivations. Most parents just want what's best for their child. This can be a healthy thing for a college-age person to recognize and articulate. This can even help relieve some of the pressure they feel. Plus, it can provide a great opportunity for us to encourage them and potentially walk with them as they seek to articulate their feelings to their parents. We can let them know that our desire is to see them get where they want to be and that we want to help them get there. And along the way we can help them discover what God wants for them, too.

What Makes You Unique?

This question really helps self-awareness. It naturally causes college-age people to differentiate themselves from everyone else, which is a crucial step in identity formulation. This can obviously give us insights into strengths they have, but it could also lead into struggles they're facing. They might feel disconnected, like nobody cares, or just completely different to the point that they have a hard time finding a sense of belonging anywhere. Again, this can provide a great opportunity for encouragement and help us discover a place where our voices can have an impact in their lives.

LAST THOUGHT

Ultimately these questions are simply a way of guiding conversation toward deeper things. But I'd encourage you to think through each of these questions yourself before you try guiding someone else through them. To help keep the conversation relaxed, you can bring up a question as one you've been asking yourself lately. Then it's simply you bringing them into your thought process. This is natural, yet it intentionally brings the relationship to deeper levels. More instruction may be necessary at times. But generally speaking, leaders need to be relaxed, guide thoughts about identity and faith, and simply be available one conversation at a time.

THE BOTTOM LINE

- Setting a relaxed tone for a conversation is of utmost importance.

- Spending time with people often has the most long-term impact.

- Asking good questions that provoke deeper conversation is usually more effective than simply giving someone information.

- We want to focus more on guiding the thoughts of others than on offering our own thoughts.

NOTES:

CHAPTER 11

STARTING AND SUSTAINING EFFECTIVE SMALL GROUPS

People desire relational connection with others who are similar to them, and small groups can be a great avenue for building these relationships. But small groups can play a role beyond that, too.

When I first wanted to start small groups in our ministry, I met with Jay[20] to talk about it. Jay grew up in the church, went to Christian school, and then walked away from the faith for a while. He started coming to our ministry with a friend and had been a part of it for about six months or so when we got together to discuss small groups. We'd hung out together quite a few times, and he wanted to help people study Scripture. As we sat at The Coffee Bean one day, we decided Jay was going to write out what he thought our small groups should be like. Letting him do that was a bit of a risk. It could be amazing, but it could also be a catastrophe.

When we're thinking about starting a small group ministry, there are all kinds of questions that come to mind: *How do we organize them? Who leads them—students or adults or both? What do they study? Do we have male and female groups, or do we include coed groups as well? How do we get leaders for these groups? How, if at all, do we train people to lead? Should small groups exist for a certain amount of time (a semester or a school year) or should they meet year-round?*

Guidelines for small groups:

1. Teach People to Study Scripture for Themselves

2. Have Leaders Facilitate Rather Than Teach

3. Bring Things Back to Everyday Life College-Age Issues

4. Form Groups out of Existing Relationships

About a week later Jay came back to me with his three-page document that answered many of these questions. Every leader will need to answer them in a way that's fitting to their context, and it was no exception for me. But Jay had thought

---

20. His name has been changed to protect his privacy.

through just about every nuance imaginable. It was amazing. We talked through the document, I pushed back on a few things, and we tweaked it a bit. We also came up with a few nonnegotiable things that we considered vital to implement in every small group. By the end of our time, we had a philosophy for small groups.

I'm still a bit surprised at how much of that original document has stuck. I've adjusted my approach and certainly my wording over the last 12 years, but not too much. Thus, I'd say there are four things that are important to integrate into small groups for college-age people.

1. TEACH PEOPLE TO STUDY SCRIPTURE FOR THEMSELVES

Unfortunately there are many people in our ministries who know biblical conclusions but don't know how to reach them on their own. They've been taught the conclusions but not how to *get* them. Consequently, the amount of time people spend studying Scripture for themselves is quite disheartening. But small groups can really make a difference in this area.

One of the nonnegotiable aspects of our small groups has always been for them to go through a book of the Bible. (That's not to say that it's wrong to do otherwise, it's just what we did.) Our heart is to have a format that inherently teaches people how to study Scripture. The best learning atmospheres are ones where we actually do what we're learning. So this lab-like approach is what I've always taken with college-age small groups.

Small group members spend time reading one section of Scripture throughout the week. Sometimes it's an entire chapter, but most often it's a few paragraphs or a section that was broken up by the translation we use. People are challenged to read the passage at least once a day over the course of the week and write down any thoughts and questions that came up as they did so. Because it's not overly time-consuming, most will come to the group having read it at least seven times. The real beauty is that they don't necessarily need someone to teach them the passage because they've repeatedly read it on their own. Certain things stood out to them, questions came to mind, and they likely saw things they'd never seen before.

Over the years I've seen a ton of benefits from this approach. First, the biggest benefit is that people begin to see value in studying Scripture. Because they were reading it over and over, they began to see something different every time. This not only showed them the depth of Scripture, but also helped them to see—after mulling it over—that they can understand it on their own. This is very different from attending a small group that's taught by someone and possibly engaging in some discussion (which is usually dominated by one or two people). With this approach everyone has already read and thought through the passage, so more group members should have something to add to the conversation.

Second, people often study passages that confirm what they know but just didn't know where it was in the Bible. This was one area where I really underestimated the impact of connecting these dots. Suddenly the group members were actually seeing—for themselves—where the conclusions they'd grown up hearing had come from. This is an important part of helping college-age people develop a faith that's truly their own.

Third, because they were spending so much time in a given passage, they could see how that passage tied into the previous week's passage. When this happens they begin to understand the author's flow of thought as well as the importance of interpreting Scripture within its context. This is perhaps the most crucial aspect of studying Scripture. And the real beauty is that we never had to teach a class on it because they were seeing it for themselves every week.

Last, this format allows more people to be involved in leading small groups. Not everyone is a teacher, so this approach expands the types of people who can lead and limits the amount of training that's necessary for them to be effective. This leads me to the next effective characteristic.

2. HAVE LEADERS FACILITATE RATHER THAN TEACH

Because people are already familiar with the passage when they come to the small group, there isn't as much of a need for the leader to be a teacher. Whoever is leading ought to know the passage and make sure the true meaning of any particular passage is known to everyone. I'd even recommend that the leader have a commentary on hand in case a question comes up during the discussion that the group cannot address on its own.

But most of the time, the leader won't have to say much at all. The leader can lead by facilitating—making sure the passage is known and applied simply through the discussion. This can be accomplished by asking basic questions such as:

- What are two things that really stood out to you in this passage?

- What do you think this teaches us about God?

- Did you see a repetition in theme or words that gave you a better understanding of what this is about?

- Were you convicted to do something because of this passage?

- As you read over the passage this week, was anything confusing to you?

- How does this section fit into what the author's been saying up to this point?

- How did this passage change or affirm your perspective on life?

The potential list of questions is limitless, but the key is that the leader facilitates rather than teaches.

Without the people even realizing it, the small group can become a lab for learning to study Scripture. People naturally learn and inevitably end up helping others learn, too. People begin to see the value of Scripture. And once this happens, we no longer need to talk about *having quiet times*. People will automatically invest their time and resources into what they find valuable. Thus, very little influence in this area is needed.

3. BRING THINGS BACK TO EVERYDAY LIFE COLLEGE-AGE ISSUES

Smaller groups of people are great avenues for deeper discussion. Understanding the basic age-stage issues that college-age people face is a key aspect of making sure they see value in Scripture. Remember, the five major areas they're working through are identity, intimacy, meaning, pleasure, and truth. You can also tack on finances, discipline, and other topics. But they ultimately fall under one of these five pursuits. So in the discussion, it's important to tie in how the passage speaks to these issues. This keeps the value of the Scripture at the front of everyone's mind.

Do this exercise yourself. Take any passage of Scripture and think through how it speaks to where (or in what) we find a sense of identity, our relationship with God or others (intimacy), what is ultimately meaningful, where we ought to find pleasure, or how it impacts what we believe. It's a fun exercise, and having a leader who's able to tie every passage back to at least one of these ideas will keep the group's discussion applicable and relevant.

4. FORM GROUPS OUT OF EXISTING RELATIONSHIPS

Instead of starting with sign-up sheets or trying to launch a small-groups campaign, consider starting groups with people who are already connected to each other. This is a great way to start—especially if you'll be using a discussion-based study like I've suggested. With this structure, you may not even need formal leaders to get small groups rolling in your ministry.

There have been many times when I've met with a group of friends for a few weeks in a row and then turned it over to them to continue on their own. First, I assigned the passage for the week. Then I told them all to read it, underline things that stood out to them, and write down any questions they might have. As we met I simply helped them realize they could do this on their own. I gave them a list of questions to ask (like the ones listed earlier), and I had them walk through those same questions every week. I also gave them the titles of some recommended commentaries and let them know that I was available to help them any time. They didn't need a leader to teach them, they just needed to dive into Scripture for themselves, talk about it, and be able to use a commentary or three in their discussions.

This can be a great solution if you're hurting for leaders. You can be available for times when they have questions, but hopefully you'll see that structuring small groups in this manner can be valuable in a lot of different ways. People will become self-feeders, which is an important part of our job description. They're learning to study Scripture on their own, and you can simply guide them toward maturity as they look into the Scripture for themselves.

Now, I want to be clear about something: I do think it's *best* to have someone lead these times, and it's ideal to have an older believer in that role. Nevertheless, this approach can still be effective, especially if you have few potential leaders.

I realize that this approach, and everything I just said, may or may not fit into the context where you serve. That determination is totally up to you and the other leaders in your church to make. But I present this approach to you as an option because it's been very effective in my ministry (much more so than just going through another book), and I believe it could be in yours as well.

AREAS TO WATCH CAREFULLY

Whichever approach you choose with your small groups, there are things to be aware of and honest about. And having these on your mind will affect whether or not you'll be successful in sustaining healthy small groups. So I want to explain four issues that I really recommend you be watchful for in the small groups you start. Of course some of these concerns apply only to some, not all, contexts and groups. But I do believe these apply to *much* more than we'd like to admit. Watch for…

In small groups watch out for:
1. Leaders Who Like to Talk a Lot
2. The Illusion of Accountability
3. Too Much Focus on Sameness
4. A Consumer Mentality

1. Leaders Who Like to Talk a Lot

One of the most unattractive things about small groups is a leader who likes to talk all the time. College-age people aren't necessarily looking for another class or a bunch of information—and they certainly aren't looking for a know-it-all leader. They desire to be a part of something that helps them learn, engages their mind, and serves as a place where they can discuss topics that are applicable to their everyday lives. So I'd recommend being very careful about who you allow to lead small groups. You can get them started with just about anyone, but sustaining it over time requires a leader who does more to help the discussion form than just impart information. And this is the case regardless of how you structure your small groups.

2. The Illusion of Accountability

We often talk about small groups as a means for bringing accountability into our lives. This can be true, but it can also be an illusion. In a small group that meets weekly, we're only accountable for those things we choose to disclose to others. This leads to small groups providing *selective accountability*, at best. These types of groups are typically more *disclosure groups* than accountability groups. People disclose only what they want the others to hold them accountable for. And even so, they can always lie about how they're doing afterward. This is disclosure, not accountability.

To clarify, I'm not saying that small groups *cannot* provide accountability. I am, however, suggesting that they don't inherently provide it like we tend to think they do.

There are a couple of practical things you can do to help bring true accountability to your small groups. Encourage those who are leading the groups to be vulnerable. The more vulnerable the leader is, the more vulnerable the other members of the group will be. Seeing vulnerability modeled in this way provides a safer environment for sharing. Also encourage leaders to give their group members permission to dig into their personal lives. The more the leader is accountable to those in the group, the more the group will have true accountability with each other.

Having group members give each other permission like this also forces issues to be addressed. For example they can talk about issues like how to respond when confronted by someone or having tact and humility when approaching someone in a confrontation. Talking about these issues provides a *ton* of teachable moments in college ministry. These conversations also address relational boundaries that many college-age people aren't aware of or used to. And this is part of the beauty of college-age small groups!

3. Too Much Focus on Sameness

Generally speaking, small groups are designed to gather similar people. This approach can be both a strength and a weakness. The strength is in peer connection. College-age people are socially driven, so this is certainly a strong point. On the other hand this can derail our goal of assimilation, if we're not careful. In order for college-age people to connect with our church as a whole, they have to be open to having relationships with people who are different from them. In other words they need to be around and relate to people who aren't the same as them. Put yet another way we need to help them embrace a healthy appreciation of differences.

By the way, this is more than a philosophy of ministry; this is at the core of the gospel. The gospel is inclusive of all types of people, not just those who are like us. So being overly focused on sameness needs to be watched closely.

Perhaps the most effective thing we can do to balance this is to have older adults lead the small groups in their own homes. The older adult (or couple) can even have their friends be a part of some discussions to make sure the college-age people are being exposed to other adults. Small groups can be a great assistance to us as we seek to expose college-age people to older adults in our church, but we need to be intentional about it. Having a lot of college-age people involved in a small group might look good on paper, but it means nothing if it stops there. A deeper connection is needed.

Another option might be starting small groups with studies on a spiritual definition of the church and how it includes all people, regardless of age, race, gender, and generation. Have the small groups start by going through passages like Ephesians 2:11-22 where there's an emphasis on Christ and the cross being the peace that brings different types of people together. Talk about the beauty of the gospel being the fact that it brings reconciliation to not only the relationship between God and humankind, but also between people. Let the group think of things they can do to live out this theology in your church. In this way you force them to think through implementing what they know, they can initiate the cause, and you can sit back and watch them seek to integrate themselves into your church based on their own study of Scripture.

You can even do things like have different people from the church come in for question-and-answer times or share from their own experience on a specific issue. Again, there are lots of things that can be done—it's just a matter of being intentional in this area.

4. A Consumer Mentality

A consumer mentality is an unhealthy focus on self. And if there's one thing that will hinder people who are different (especially from different generations) from having a relationship and serving each other, it's a consumer mentality. Unfortunately small groups can feed this unhealthy focus. We don't usually think about this, but it's true.

People go to small groups for what they can get out of it—for *their* lives. They go to *get* something. The motivation for going is self-focused. In our culture this is acceptable and applauded. People talk about needing to be *fed*, and if they don't feel like they're getting what they need, they leave. This consumer mentality can be a huge hindrance to developing mature believers who remain a part of our churches.

And by the way, as a not-so-side note, the gospel message at its very core is anti-consumer. Christ is extremely clear about the fact that those who follow him have to deny themselves.[21] This is anything but a consumer mentality.

Now, I'm fully aware that there are lots of other things that feed a consumer mentality—just about everything in our culture does. But we have to recognize and battle this in our small groups. We can do this by watching two very simple things. First, make sure your leaders genuinely serve others and provide great models for people to follow. Remember, college-age people don't necessarily need another study as much as they need to watch and follow the example of others. This is what assists them in turning information into wisdom. Having leaders who live out what they know is much more effective than having arrogant and self-centered brainiacs. Harsh, but true.

Second, focus on service in your small groups. Walk through passages that emphasize serving the needy and helpless and then serve in a variety of ways together. Plug into what other groups in your church are already doing and join them in their service work. This not only helps fight the consumer mentality with service, but it also encourages connections with others in the church. Let college-age people come up with ideas for how to serve people in your church and city. And then actually do them.

GETTING A GOOD START

To summarize this section, here is a short list of things I'd recommend doing *before* you launch small groups:

- Talk through these issues with your small group leaders. Discuss each one as a potential concern and talk about keeping an eye out for the slightest appearance of any of them.

- Talk about how leaders can intentionally do things to ensure that their groups don't go down these paths. Use some of the practical examples I gave you as starting points, but come up with some other possibilities as a group.

---

21. Luke 9:23. Also look at the end of this chapter, verses 57-62, for what Christ requires of those who say they will follow him.

- Make sure small group leaders are thinking beyond their individual groups and viewing that time as a means to a greater end—connection to the church as a whole. Make sure you discuss practical ways the small groups can help the goal of assimilation into the church.

Again, small groups can be a very effective part of your ministry, and they can even help you in your goal of connecting college-age people to the life of your church. But you need to watch certain tendencies and be intentional.

THE BOTTOM LINE

- Small groups can be a great vehicle for helping people study Scripture for themselves.

- Conversation-based groups are usually more effective than teacher-pupil groups.

- Every study we do should tie in to one of the five major college-age issues (identity, intimacy, meaning, pleasure, and truth).

- People usually join these groups for relational connection, so starting groups around existing relationships is ideal.

- To have groups that are effective and sustainable, we need to carefully watch four things: Leaders who like to talk a lot, whether or not we actually have accountability, an unhealthy focus on sameness, and enabling a consumer mentality.

NOTES:

CHAPTER 12
SHIFTS IN TEACHING APPROACHES

When my mom used to tell me to do something, I'd often ask, "Why?" And she'd immediately respond, "Because I said so." There was never room for discussion. And if I questioned her further, there was a price to pay. It was very clear that when she told us kids to do something, we were fully expected to just do it. No questions, no pushback, no need for explanation—or else!

This approach to parenting is important in many different ways. I have two children, so I understand that if I give either of my girls an inch, they'll try to take a mile. If I ask them to do something, I also expect them to just do it. And, like my mom, I don't find it appropriate for them to challenge me. I expect them to follow through with what I ask, when I ask them. I'm trying to teach my girls life lessons, and obedience is a vital one—especially from a Christian perspective. Trying to rationalize with them, at ages five and two, as to why I'm asking them to do something is somewhat ridiculous. But as they get older, I know there will be a certain amount of appropriateness to my explaining those things so they can understand the issues at a deeper level—and definitely so when it comes to faith issues.

> College-age people are at a point in their lives where they're questioning all of the assumptions they grew up with. And faith is no exception.

College-age people are at a point in their lives where they're questioning all of the assumptions they grew up with. In other words they're processing through whether or not they believe all the lessons their parents taught them. Many will stick, but all are challenged to one degree or another. And faith is no exception. It's a good and natural process at this age, and we need to be sure that our approach to teaching fits the life stage of the people we minister to.

FIVE MAJOR SHIFTS IN TEACHING APPROACHES

When we're teaching children about God, we need to be fairly black-and-white in our approach. Their minds are limited when it comes to abstract abilities, so we have to be very literal in our teaching. We have to avoid gray areas.

But college-age people are different.

Very different.

This is why I've found that shifting our approach to teaching in five specific ways greatly increases our effectiveness with college-age people. So I want to walk through them with you and offer some thoughts as to the importance of each shift.

Five shifts for effectively teaching college-age people:
1. From Conclusions to Assumptions
2. From Indoctrinating to Imparting Wisdom
3. From Behavioral to Spiritual Focus
4. From Giving to Equipping
5. From Telling to Shaping

1. From Conclusions to Assumptions

Every church has some kind of doctrinal statement. It's basically a list of all the conclusions the church has come to regarding major theological issues. In the church we typically teach these conclusions fairly well. We deliver messages on them, we offer classes, and the major issues are usually peppered throughout small-group discussions, class materials, and Sunday morning sermons. Consequently kids grow up learning what *we* believe. I believe this is one of the biggest reasons why college-age people walk away from the church after high school graduation: They're leaving with *our* conclusions, not their own personal faith.

Junior high and high school ministries seek to help in this matter, but even then we can fall into a rut of simply teaching our conclusions. If we want young people to have *their own* faith, then at some point we'll need to help them understand the assumptions we embrace that lead to the conclusions we hold so dearly.

For instance I personally believe in the deity of Christ—Christ is God in the flesh—and I can point to various passages in the Bible that lead me to believe this. I've clearly concluded in my own belief system that God came to the earth as a human being named Jesus. But there is a lot that I *assume* to be true that allows me to reach that conclusion. I first have to assume there is a God. I also have to assume that the Scriptures I'm reading are in fact God's words. I have to assume the version of the Bible I'm reading is accurate. And I'm assuming a person named Jesus actually lived on the earth.

My point is that I cannot come to the conclusion I did without first assuming all of these things to be true. And helping people think through the necessary assumptions will eventually allow them to personally embrace our conclusions as their own.

Sound like a lot of work? Well, it is in a way, but not as much as you might think. Just think about shifting your focus a little. Instead of teaching the conclusions and showing people where they are in the Bible, we should help them think through the assumptions *behind* the conclusions by asking them a few questions. Challenging people to do this is a great way to engage their minds and help them formulate a faith of their own.

For example you can ask a group of people if they believe Jesus is God. If they respond positively, simply ask why they believe that. Typically they know the conclusion. But if you ask them why, you'll likely see them squirm a little. If they respond with something like, "The Bible says so," then you can push back by asking, "Okay, give me three places where the Bible says that."

To put this as simply as I can, instead of just articulating theological conclusions, we can require people to process through these things at a much deeper level by asking the "Why?" questions.

2. From Indoctrinating to Imparting Wisdom

Indoctrination is a fancy way of saying we teach people what we believe from an information standpoint—and at times we even tell them how to apply that information to their lives. Church leaders have traditionally been good at giving good and concise information through classes, small-group studies, and sermons. But imparting wisdom is different.

If indoctrination is giving information, then imparting wisdom is showing how that information is lived out. An indoctrinated person knows information; a wise person is deeply committed to living out what they know. In chapter 9 of *College Ministry 101*, I shared about a guy in my college ministry named

James. He was a great kid and well liked by most. We were sitting down for coffee one day, and he told me straight-out that he was bored with God and with church. He wasn't bitter or frustrated; he was genuinely bored. I asked him why he thought he was bored, and he simply responded, "I'm just sick of going to church."

Eventually James explained that his entire Christian life revolved around the church campus where Bible studies were held and church events hosted. He was saturated by church culture and knew a lot of biblical information. He went from one Bible study or gathering to the next, and eventually he got bored—who wouldn't? At the same time, he was living life by his own rules. He wasn't living an outlandish lifestyle, but he wasn't living a Christlike life either.

At the end of our conversation, I looked him straight in the eyes and said, "You're right—your life is boring. Your problem is that you're a smart guy, and you know a lot of information, but you don't obey any of it." Just so you know, I'm not always that forward with people, but our relationship warranted it, and he needed to hear it. I went even further, "I wonder if it would be so boring if you started living out what you know—if you were able to say you knew things from experience, rather than just regurgitating what you've been told." He was a little taken aback, but he understood what I was saying.

Rather than teaching more information, consider shifting your focus to help people become deeply committed to what they already know. Much more than complex discussion or giving more information, teaching college-age people is about encouraging deep commitment to simple truths. I'm not suggesting you abandon teaching new information, nor would I say we shouldn't talk about the deeper concepts of faith. I'm simply suggesting a shift in focus to intentionally help people embrace truth in their lives to the point where they *feel* and experience all the pressures of living it out. Why would we give out more information if people aren't living out what we've already given to them? It's through the experience of living out truth that wisdom is gained.

At this point it may not surprise you that I'd suggest that connecting college-age people with older, spiritually maturing adults is one of the best ways to do this. We need to connect them with people who actually live out their beliefs in life—and preferably people who've been doing so for some time. So by concentrating on connecting college-age people to the lives of older believers in your church, you can do more than just give them a sense of belonging in the church. You can also meet their most immediate needs of faith development by imparting wisdom through the life experience of others.

3. From Behavioral to Spiritual Focus

James 1:22 issues a command to believers to be doers of the word, not only hearers of it. In fact the entire book of James challenges believers to *do* something with what we know. This is an extremely important aspect of our faith. The last thing the church needs is a bunch of people calling themselves Christians and not doing anything about it in the world.

But in some ways we've become out of balance—focusing too much on behavior and ignoring what *actually produces* the behavior. Jesus confronts the Pharisees in Matthew 22:37-39, saying the greatest command is to love God with all their hearts, all their souls, and all their minds. He quotes a passage of Scripture from Deuteronomy 6—one these people knew inside and out. After all they had it on the doorposts of their homes and even wore this section of Scripture around their arms and foreheads when they prayed. But they missed something—it's called *the point*. They knew the information, but they lost the heart of it. The Pharisees were good, moral, church-going people who *did* all the right things. But there was a need for something deeper, and this is where Jesus confronts them on multiple occasions. (For example see Matthew 23:23-36.)

I love the insight that 1 Thessalonians 1:3 gives us on this issue. The apostle Paul is writing to people in the church at Thessalonica. He says he remembers "your work produced by faith, your labor prompted by love, and your endurance inspired by hope in our Lord Jesus Christ." In the Greek language the emphasis is clearly on the faith, love, and hope of Paul's audience. In fact the way Paul structures his sentence stresses that these three qualities *produce* their work, labor, and endurance. The *NIV* version uses different terms such as *prompted* and *inspired* for reading purposes, but the literal meaning in Greek is *produced*. The Thessalonian believers' spirituality was producing outward action, not vice versa. Outward actions are simply markers of our spiritual condition. We can try to get people to move in a behavioral direction; but in order to be truly effective, we have to go much deeper. We must develop people's faith, love, and hope. And when we do, the outward actions take care of themselves (Matthew 23:25-26).

Consider talking about spiritual truths without giving behavioral application. I know that may be difficult at first because it's not typically our approach, but try having people think and pray through the application points for themselves. Force them to think through these things beyond the all-too-typical "Sunday school answers." Make sure they don't just regurgitate what they've heard growing up but are really thinking through it for themselves.

4. From Giving to Equipping

Our traditional approach to teaching has been that the preacher does a ton of study in a passage of Scripture, formulates conclusions on that passage using Bible study methods, thinks about how the passage applies to the lives of those who will listen to the message, and then packages the message into approximately 30 minutes. It's well prepared and concise. I believe the time spent creating a message is necessary because when we give a message, we ought to know the passage and have thought through it well.

But what about everyone else? Shouldn't they be able to think through it, too?

Way too often people sit in our churches and hear conclusions based on someone else's study of Scripture. They go home with no idea of how to study it for themselves. They're *given* a message discussing Scripture, but they aren't necessarily *equipped* to get truth out of Scripture on their own.

College-age people are no exception. Consider shifting your focus from giving the conclusions of your study to equipping others to draw their own conclusions. You can still teach a passage of Scripture; but as you do, share about how you came to that conclusion. Share about your study process; tell them what stood out to you and why. There are all kinds of resources on basic Bible study methods that you can refer to, but letting people into your personal process can be even more effective. If you're going to guide people toward Christlikeness, then they must be able to study Scripture. Shifting your focus from giving information to equipping others to get it for themselves is what's needed.

5. From Telling to Shaping

As Christians we're to seek a biblical worldview. By that I mean we desire to view the world through the eyes of Scripture. We're trying to view things the way God does. In one way or another, our doctrinal statements, classes, small groups, and sermons tell our worldview. But these things don't necessarily shape the worldview of others.

College-age people are in the midst of developing a worldview of their own. Even if they've been around the church for a while, they don't necessarily have a biblical worldview. This shift might seem a little less drastic than the others, but consider being intentional about shaping other people's worldview more than telling them your own.

Consider being intentional about shaping other people's worldview more than telling them your own.

There are some very practical things I do to help in this, but one thing I always seek to do is compare the message of a particular passage with the American norm in that area. For instance in Luke 14:26 Jesus says, "If anyone comes to me and does not hate father and mother, wife and children, brothers and sisters—yes, even life itself—such a person cannot be my disciple." Now comparing that to the American norm is clearly a conflict. So much so, in fact, that we have a hard time understanding what Jesus is saying. This is because it's a clash of worldviews.

As Americans we place an extremely high value on family and can hardly grasp why Jesus wouldn't do the same. But in order to understand what Jesus is saying, we have to view the things of the world—including family—the way Jesus does. Then, and only then, will this passage make sense to us. My point is clearly not to write a commentary on this particular passage, but rather to demonstrate how the way we view the world drastically affects our understanding of Scripture.

When you teach, consider seeking to shape a biblical worldview in people, rather than simply teaching them yours. Bring out passages like this one from Luke 14 and talk about the different perspectives. Discuss different ways of viewing this passage and get people thinking about Jesus' perspective when he makes this statement. Then compare that to the American norm. Does Jesus not value family? Or does he have a deeper perspective that we miss? By asking these types of questions and discussing passages in this way, we can help people shape a worldview of their own.

And, by the way, it also makes our time together more intriguing for the college-age mind. It stretches them. It forces them to think more deeply. Perhaps most importantly, they're not bored by a sermon that gives them three simple points they don't really have to think about. Instead, they're being pushed both intellectually and practically.

THE BOTTOM LINE

- College-age people are thinking critically, and we need to embrace this.

- We must help people develop and form a foundation of their own.

- We have to help people live out what they know.

- Spiritual aspects are what drive physical behavior, so we must work on the former.

- Shaping worldview is more important than telling people our own.

NOTES:

CHAPTER 13

SEVEN CRITICAL TEACHING TOPICS

I frequently get emails from people asking about good teaching topics for their ministries. I get very excited about people who want to guide college-age people toward biblically mature conclusions in the five general issues they're facing. So I happily respond!

It's that kind of heart and passion that leads me to write this chapter. I want to discuss some topics that I've found to be vital for any leader of a college-age ministry to address. And this isn't limited to traditional settings like small groups, discussion groups, or sermons. Keep these topics in mind during one-on-one conversations as well.

Teaching on any of the broad issues of identity, intimacy, meaning, pleasure, or truth is going to be good. But I'd like to be even more detailed here, giving you specific topics to teach on and why. My hope is that walking through these things will ignite even more ideas and creativity in you.

Some of the topics may seem very basic, and many of them are commonly taught in student ministries as well. But even when they seem repetitive, they're important to discuss with your college-age people because—

- College-age people think much more abstractly than they did when they were in junior high and high school. Thus, they'll process through the topic very differently now from when they studied it before.

- Much of what they've learned they haven't yet applied to their lives, so discussing these things again and helping them process through the implications (and possibly assumptions) for each area is very healthy.

- These are issues we all need to hear repeatedly—regardless of our age or stage.

- College-age people will sift through these areas in ways that are different from people in other age stages. As I've said earlier, this is a unique stage of life dealing with unique pressures and challenges which requires us to be very specific.

So here is a short list of seven topics to cover in your ministry. I hope it will give you some direction and inspire your own ideas. The list is followed by more information on why each is important and teaching ideas to get you started:

1. Shame and Guilt

2. Relationships

3. The Bible

4. Identity

5. Finances

6. Faithfulness

7. Controversial Topics

TOPIC 1: SHAME AND GUILT

If we don't grasp an understanding of God's grace and mercy, we're in big trouble. Dealing with shame and guilt is the number one reason so many people slip into mediocre Christianity. Shame from sin causes people to disengage from the body of Christ and ministry. So if we want to help college-age people connect with the body, we have to help them understand this issue.

Shame over our sin causes us to run and hide from God—and usually the things of God—just like Adam and Eve did in the garden (Genesis 3:8). It's when we don't understand the theology of a sinful nature in the context of God's grace that our view of God gets tweaked. We need to offer a theological perspective on this, helping college-age people understand that it's not okay to sin, but the fact that they do sin makes them normal. And most importantly, we need to help them realize that where there is repentance, there's also freedom. If we don't, then connection to the body of Christ will be lost.

- *Free.* There are a number of different passages that apply here, but a good one to start with is Psalm 51. David wrote this Psalm after Nathan confronted him regarding his adulterous encounter with Bathsheba (2 Samuel 11–12). In this Psalm we see David's ownership of his sin (verses 1-6), we see him ask for cleansing and forgiveness (verses 7-12), and then we see his freedom (verses 13-19).[22]

- *Forgiven.* Another great passage is Romans 7:14–8:1. A talk from this passage can deal with wrongly identifying ourselves in sin, rather than who God has made us to be in Christ. There are a couple of different times when Paul separates his identity from his sin. In fact in verses 17 and 20 he says that when he does things he doesn't want to do (sinful things), it's no longer *him* doing it but the sin within him. He separates his true identity from his sin and views himself as he is—completely accepted by God because of what Jesus accomplished (7:25–8:1).

TOPIC 2: RELATIONSHIPS

Relationships are sought in completely new ways during the college-age years. If this topic isn't covered at least annually, then a core issue of this stage of life will be missed. Late adolescents have a unique desire for intimacy in relationships—both healthy same-sex friendships, as well as friendships and dating relationships with the opposite sex. This topic is necessary for preparation and guidance purposes. We want to make sure they're spending their energy preparing themselves for godly relationships, rather than looking for the *prepared one.* This is a vital point. Far too often college-age people are seeking the "right person," rather than *becoming* the "right person."

---

22. If you'd like to refer to the notes I used when I taught on this passage, go to http://www.collegeleader.org/resources.php.

There are many areas to address in a series on relationships. Some that I've put into a series include:

- *Homosexuality.*[23] I've taught through passages of Scripture and explained the differences in opinion from the most conservative to the most liberal. Addressing this topic in your ministry is a must. It's a huge issue that college-age people deal with, and you have the opportunity to teach and model a proper biblical response to someone who struggles. Be prepared for people to admit their struggles with this issue. Even if they aren't personally dealing with it, many know someone who is. This topic is extremely intriguing— and emotionally charged. Be wise with your words, hold firm to your convictions, and be gracious to those who desire change.

- *Marriage.* I've put together a message series on this topic called "Relationships by Design."[24] In it I talk about God's design for marriage, God-given roles in marriage, and steps for preparing for these things.

- *Beauty.* Another series I've done is called "What Makes a Woman Beautiful?"[25] I've taught on this topic a few times, and I've had women in our church do so as well.

- *Song of Songs.*[26] I break down this book of the Bible by sections and talk through the different aspects of the relationship from dating, the wedding night, and on into marriage.

TOPIC 3: THE BIBLE

This topic is massive for college-age people. Most who've grown up in church feel as though they already know the Bible. They've likely had some sort of teaching on what the Bible is, but there are many who can't answer some of the most basic questions asked in culture today. *Why do we have the 66 books of the Bible, and what makes them God-inspired over all other writings?*

---

23. For resources and information on this topic, check out: http://www.exodusinternational.org/. I also taught a message about this issue on April 17, 2005, during a service at Cornerstone. To listen to that, go to: http://www.cornerstonesimi.com/special/media_player.html.

24. For a resource to help you teach on this topic, go to: http://collegeleader.org/store/.

25. For a free, downloadable small-group study on this, go to: http://www.collegeleader.org/resources.php.

26. For a resource to help you teach on this topic, go to: http://collegeleader.org/store/.

How did we even get these books? What about contradictions in the Bible? How do we know that the Bible we have is accurate to the original writings?

There are a wide variety of issues to focus on under this topic, and some take more expertise than others. If you have training (or can find someone in your church who does), then you might want to tackle subjects like the ancient process the scribes used in copying Scripture, the Dead Sea Scrolls, or differences in the Greek and Hebrew meanings of words.

But you don't have to have an advanced degree to teach on the Bible. There are great books available, such as Josh McDowell's *Evidence That Demands a Verdict* or *A Ready Defense*, that provide a ton of information. Another book you can use is *When Skeptics Ask* by Ronald Brooks and Norman L. Geisler. But however you approach it, addressing this issue of a skeptic is good. We have to address the questions that the average person might have when it comes to the Bible.

Now you may think people already know this stuff, but trust me—most don't! In fact most don't even know simple Bible study methods, so they rarely read the Bible. Here's a list of topics you can teach on using books like the ones I mentioned above:

- Inspiration—what we believe about the Scriptures

- The Formation—why the 66 books, how we got them, and so on

- Preservation of Scripture over the years—dealing with criticism

- Rhyme and Reason—explaining that there is logic in believing what we do

- Dealing with Contradictions—walk through seemingly contradictory passages and explain how and why they might vary from each other at first glance

- How to get more out of the Bible—discuss and demonstrate simple Bible study methods

- Why we need the Bible—what God intended for the Scriptures to do in our lives

TOPIC 4: IDENTITY[27]

Finding a sense of identity solely in Christ is a struggle for all of us. But to a college-age person, the search for identity goes to an entirely different level. Many college-age people are at the stage where they realize they have no firm identity but are desperately seeking one—both in society as well as spiritually. With their high school identity in the past, they pursue a new identity with intensity.

Unfortunately, due to pressure from parents and other adults to find a career path, they tend to put most of their energy into finding an identity in society. Parents ask their kids, "What are you going to do with your life?" As they look to other adults who are settled into a career or family life, college-age people are in a state of wonder as to where they'll land in these arenas. They have dreams and aspirations, but most lack a sense of direction as to how to get there. It's vital that we understand their inner struggles as we work with them.

The goal of teaching on this topic is not to get people to find a sociological identity in a career, but to help them embrace their spiritual identity in Christ *before* they find an identity in society.[28] If there's ever a teachable moment where the topic of identity can be capitalized on, then the college-age stage of life is it. When we talk through this issue, it automatically goes straight to the heart.

I personally believe that everything ultimately comes back to an identity issue. Who or what we identify ourselves in will drive every aspect of our lives. So I weave this topic pretty much into all of my messages and conversations. Here are a few ideas for teaching on this subject:

- *Identity: Beyond the Crowd.* Although we can never completely separate our identity as Christians from the body of Christ, we still must have a *personal* relationship with Jesus. The goal of this message is to push people to question whether they have a relationship with church events and gatherings or personally with Christ. A lot of people would *say* they have a relationship with Jesus; but on closer self-examination, they find there isn't much of one outside of church-organized events and gatherings. College-age people really struggle with this—especially those who've grown

---

27. I've done a helpful small-group video series on this topic called Who Am I? For more on that, go to: http://collegeleader.org/store/.

28. For a more complete discussion on this issue and the stages people go through during the college-age years, see chapter 2 of *College Ministry 101*.

up in church. One way to approach this would be to look at Jesus' response to the religious routing and hypocrisy of the Pharisees in Matthew 23 and compare it to our own lives and the church today. Verses 23-28 are a good place to focus as the comparisons come easily.

• *Identity: In the World.* As I mentioned earlier, the number one ingredient to a mediocre Christian life is wrongfully identifying ourselves in sin struggles, rather than in Christ. Identity in shame causes many to shrink back from truly pursuing a relationship with Christ or engaging in ministry and the life of the church. Use 1 Peter 2:4-12 to get people thinking about God's view of our identity in the world. The goal of the message is to give people freedom in Christ and to help them understand that finding identity in Christ means we belong in the body of Christ. And it's belonging to the body that gives us an identity in the world—wherever that may be.

• *Identity: Beyond Circumstances.* College-age people are reevaluating all of their childhood assumptions when it comes to faith. Consequently many don't have an identity in spiritual truths, so they run to a career, ministry role, or relationship to get that immediate sense of belonging. This is what we want to protect them from, because these sociological things always seem to change. And when that change inevitably comes, it leaves the individual searching for yet another identity. Our identity must be found outside of circumstances (good or bad). Choose Scripture like Ephesians 1:1-14 to help people think through their identity in Christ—beyond their circumstances.

• *Identity: Beyond the American Dream.* Owning a home, having a family, and having a good-paying job to support yourself are what we consider to be the "American dream." However, by "support yourself" Americans typically mean "give me everything I want so I never have to struggle financially." This identity search is not only empty, but it's flat-out wrong. So this talk seeks to stretch college-age people to the point where they move past this American standard of success to a point of contentment—a place where they're okay with doing anything God has for them. Luke 9:57-62 can serve as a great discussion starter as you work through what God calls us to commit to when we follow him. We must be careful that we don't create or add to any bitterness that college-age people may feel toward their parents—even as we challenge the typical standard that many parents place on their kids. If there's ever a topic that will get the attention of your college-age friends, this is it. They feel a tremendous amount of pressure in this area, and you could be the breath of fresh air they need.

TOPIC 5: FINANCES[29]

Financial trouble is an all-too-prevalent pitfall during the college-age years. Poor financial decisions made between the ages of 18 and 25 usually don't have to be paid for until later—which is what often contributes to the financial canyons that many people dig for themselves. When we teach on this topic, we need to hit it dead-on. We need to be bold, encouraging discipline in this area and being honest about the consequences if there isn't.

Talking through the parable of the talents (Matthew 25:14-30) is a great way to launch weeks (literally) of discussion on this issue. It hits tensions that we all face when it comes to money. Two main ones to cover are—

- *Giving Today*. The guy who brought back ten talents was honored. Typically we take this passage *completely* out of context, suggesting that this gives us the freedom to invest our money with the hope of multiplying it *for ourselves*. The man in this passage, however, didn't keep anything for himself. He multiplied it and gave it *all* back to the master. The main reason why people pursue a college education is so they can make more money. But for who? Challenge your listeners to think honestly about whether they're giving it all to the Master now. If they aren't giving it all now, then they certainly won't do it later—even though they probably think they will. Encourage faithfulness with their money today as the foundation for faithfulness later in life.

- *The Issue of Debt*. The guy who ended up with the one talent he'd been given was shamed and deemed unfaithful. If our Master came back today, the reality is that most college-age people wouldn't even have what was given to them. They'd be handing the Master a bill. And some would hand him a very large one. The guy in this passage didn't have any debt; he actually brought the master something. Yet he was still viewed as unfaithful.

---

29. For a free downloadable handout and talk notes on this topic, go to: http://www.collegeleader.org/resources.php.

These points hit all of us to some degree, but they can really hit home for college-age people (especially those who are going into debt for their schooling). But one thing is certain: You'll initiate some great discussions with this topic. Be prepared for your students to ask you how *you* spend and use your money *for the Master*. Be prepared for them to question whether they should have a savings account, or if it's wrong to take out loans for school. These questions are tough ones, but the discussion and life transformation they can ignite are exciting.

This can be a great way of forcing your students to think biblically. Our American mindset can easily take over, rationalizing away a biblical perspective on finances. This topic, and particularly this passage, will open up a HUGE can of worms! But it's worth it.

Do all you can to make it practical and personal—be upfront about how you manage and prioritize your finances, as well as the struggles you've faced. Consider having people who've weathered financial problems in the past or present come and share the pain they've faced because of their poor decisions. And use the resources of people in your church who know a lot about this topic or who are living faithfully to share examples of what it looks like to do it right. You may even want to get more practical and have someone show your group how to set up and maintain a budget.

TOPIC 6: FAITHFULNESS

Thinking about what the future holds can be an all-consuming venture for college-age people. As they look forward to what's to come, there are feelings of hope, excitement, and anxiety. Obtaining a college degree is essentially a hoop that needs to be jumped through in our culture. It's something we must do in order to have any hope of landing a solid career path. But as college students are moving through this time in their lives, visions of the future can easily cause them to lose sight of what's important today.

Even if they don't attend school, they're in a stage of life that's transitory in nature. So talking about faithfulness today—where they are, here and now—is a never-ending job. The list of areas in which we need to be faithful is endless—academics, witness on campus or in the workplace, finances, and pursuing holiness. But the underlying issue that needs to be addressed is faithfulness *today*. A couple of areas to focus on include—

- *Worry.* I don't know about you, but whenever I'm consumed with what's to come, I end up feeling discontented with today—and thus I'm unfaithful. There's something to Jesus' command not to worry about tomorrow, for tomorrow will worry about itself (Matthew 6:25-34). For me, this rings all too true. I often see this in college-age people, too. They're so focused on what's to come or where they're heading that they lose sight of the fact that God has them where they are—today. One of the hardest balances in this college-age time of life is working toward the future while being faithful and content with where they are today.

- *Excellence.* Helping college-age people be faithful even in their studies is an important part of our ministry.[30] Part of our role is helping them understand that although this is a time of preparation, God has still called them to be faithful to him today. He still desires them to be Christlike, He still wants them to honor him in all things. And if God is calling them to a particular field or industry, then they ought to seek to excel in that area and use it as their God-given mission field. Far too many college students don't connect the dots on this issue, but it's an important part of being faithful. Use Scripture like Colossians 3:17 to drive home the point that God has called them to be faithful and to do everything—including studying—in the name of Jesus.

TOPIC 7: CONTROVERSIAL TOPICS

All of the above topics are great to touch on, but perhaps some of the most intriguing for people are those without clear-cut answers. Since college-age people are thinking through all sorts of things, it can be fun to stretch the conversations a bit. Be careful not to allow people to major on the minor issues too much and be watchful of any divisive conversation. But don't avoid topics that can ignite deeper thought. Talk with the leadership of your church to be sure everyone is on the same page with the purpose of having college-age people explore these topics, and then dive right in.

Here are some topics I've found to be great to teach through, where discussions carry on for days and weeks afterward:

---

30. For a resource that students can read—or you can use to gain some insights into this issue—see Donald Opitz and Derek Melleby's book, *The Outrageous Idea of Academic Faithfulness.*

- *Spiritual Gift of Tongues.* Always a heated topic, it's often an issue of debate and wonder with college-age people. Take time to sift through the passages that deal with this issue and break down both schools of thought. Try not to tell your own view, but seek to do each side justice. You may even want to put together handouts describing both views for people to review. Pull your information from the authors themselves and put the full arguments into the hands of your students. It takes a bit of work and study on your end, but it can be a lot of fun.

- *Predestination.* Again, just as above, teach through passages that deal with this issue and give both sides. Commentaries on particular passages can be very helpful. Just be sure you present both sides, walking through each view clearly and simply. Then watch the conversations go.

- *Other World Religions.* Other religions and belief systems have a huge influence on college-age people's concept of truth. So covering this topic is important. There are lots of possible series titles, but I think my favorite was "Distinctions"—an approach that showed how each belief system is *distinct* from a Protestant Christian faith. You can discuss Roman Catholicism, Baha'i, Jehovah's Witnesses, Mormonism, Buddhism, Islam, Hinduism, you name it. By doing a simple Internet search, you can find books on just about any faith system. Again, this takes some work on your end to prepare or find an expert. But I'd recommend that you make sure you understand the faith and their arguments against Christianity (using their exact wording from *their* books), and you should also be able to walk through these ideas and arguments with your students. Present the information in as unbiased an approach as possible. Simply present how they're distinct and then facilitate the discussion. If you have a smaller group of students, you can even do the research with them. Be prepared—some people might get a little fired up. But sometimes that's half the fun.

THE BOTTOM LINE

• We want to cover topics well but encourage deep commitment to the simple things.

• College-age people must learn to understand that they're called to be faithful today, regardless of what God may do tomorrow.

NOTES:

CHAPTER 14

MISSION TRIPS—WHAT TO INCLUDE AND WHY

My first trip overseas was to scout out an organization for a potential mission trip to Romania. A friend of a friend knew someone who had friends going to visit a ministry over there. Yeah, if that sounds confusing, that's because it is. The point is that I went to Romania to visit an organization that worked with orphans. I wanted to see if this would be a good place to take college-age people over the summer, and I was absolutely blown away by what I experienced there.

One of the darkest places I've ever visited was an orphanage just outside Oradea. It was a run-down building with no heat or warm water. When I was there, there was snow on the ground. And it was so cold inside this place that if there hadn't been a roof, then there would have been snow inside the building as well. The hallways were long, dark, and damp. The building was filled with an aroma of horrible food, filth, dampness, and about 100 high school aged kids who had no concept of hygiene.

As we learned about these teenagers and their situation, it became even more disheartening. They were totally abused, even raped by the employees, extremely malnourished, and oppressed by the director. The amount of corrupt activity in this place was more sickening than the fact that it was the middle of winter and these kids had no heat and had to take freezing cold showers.

The physical and emotional scars were apparent.

The smell was unavoidable.

And after talking with the kids, it was impossible not to fall in love with them.

We also went to another place, which, believe it or not, had a history of being even worse. Well, at least in my mind. This was a place for infants. The babies were kept in steel cribs with plywood bottoms. Some had blankets to lie on. But most were just lying on top of the bare wood, and they had splinters in the backs of their heads. They also had scabs on their arms and bodies—caused by the rats chewing on them during the night. They were given one bottle a day and changed once a day. In other words, they were touched only once a day. The stench from dirty diapers was horrible. But even worse was the eerie silence. These babies had learned that crying doesn't help—nobody comes to help them when they cry. So they just lay there in their dirty diapers, hungry, with nobody to love or nurture them.

It was horrifying to see.

Thankfully the organization we went to visit was seriously tackling so many of these issues—and as of today, it has made tremendous changes. The orphanage for older kids has been shut down, and they've taken over the place for infants, making sure they get the care and nurture they need—and deserve. Volunteers from around the world have given their entire lives to love on these orphaned children, making sure they can have as normal a life as possible. The organization even developed an adoption program out of that nursery, stopping these kids from going into the corrupt state-run orphanage system. Unfortunately that program had to be adjusted when the Romanian government sought to be a part of the European Union. Politics had a drastic negative impact, no longer allowing adoptions to occur. But despite these setbacks, the organization is doing their best at protecting these children from further heartbreak and mistreatment.

On this scouting trip my wife, Barbara, and I went from one place to the next with this group of people. Our hearts were both broken and encouraged. But deep down I knew this was going to be a great place to take college-age people. They needed to see this. Every one of them. I believed with all of my heart that it was going to change their lives.

And I was right.

> Our hearts were both broken and encouraged. But deep down, I knew this was going to be a great place to take college-age people. They needed to see this. Every one of them.

PLANNING

Along the way we took pictures and lots of notes. We talked with the leaders of this organization about what the trip might look like. We had a ton of ideas, a tentative schedule in place, and a two-week block of time when we were planning to bring a team back to Romania. We went home very excited about exposing our students to all that we'd seen.

I've found that doing a scouting trip beforehand is most beneficial. It isn't always possible, but I highly recommend it. It really helps to have been to the location before leading other people there. Plus, having personal experience and pictures and stories really helps people understand what the trip is going to be about.

At that time the organization could house only about 20 people. So with my wife and me going, that meant about 17 to 18 students could go (depending on whether or not other adults came along). I put together an application for people to fill out, and I announced in November that we'd be taking a trip to Romania the next summer. I explained the heart of the trip and had the applications available. We told them that since the trip was in June, we'd have the team members chosen by the end of December because team meetings would begin in January.

There was such a positive response that we had to turn away dozens of people. You might think it's because I'm such a great salesman. Nope. I firmly believe it was because we were able to show a way that they could have an impact and be a part of doing good in the world.

Give college-age people a cause to live for, and they'll go for it.

We put together a team of people and began planning. During the first meeting, we went through the usual stuff: A timeline for fundraising, a bit of training on writing a support letter, information regarding immunizations and passports, basic details about the trip, and materials that covered some cultural aspects that we needed to be aware of. It was a great time, and we prayed for each other and for the people there. We met every three to four weeks. And then during the month prior to the trip, we met every week for planning and organizational purposes. There are always a ton of details that go into these trips, and keeping everything organized is crucial to the success of it.

This trip was to last a total of two weeks and purposefully so. The first week was all about learning and being exposed to the ministry and culture. Every day we saw different aspects of the ministry and did things to understand both traditional Romanian culture as well as that of the orphanages. It's very different. We learned and saw how orphans were treated and viewed in that culture. This first week proved to be totally worth the time because the second week we put together a summer camp for some of the kids in an orphanage. We got permission to take them out of the orphanage and up to a place in the mountains where we spent five nights with them. We could love them, have fun, share about Christ, and make sure they had three solid meals a day. It was such a blessing—for us and for the kids.

KEEP DOING THE THINGS THAT WORKED

No matter how we looked at it, we thought the trip was a success. From this very first mission team, we even had four people who eventually moved to Romania as missionaries. It was an extremely powerful time for our ministry and church. And one really fun aspect was the fact that after hearing our stories, the college-age people in our ministry fully funded those four to go back and serve. We even had older adults ask if they could go on the trip the following year. It was truly amazing.

The next few years we did two separate trips for two weeks each, with two teams in each group for a total of four teams. During the first week, one team was exposed to the culture and ministry, while the other team put on the camp for kids. Then during the following week, they'd

> In mission trips with college-age people, I highly recommend that you make sure these three aspects—exposure, service, and relationships—are at the core of every part of every trip you do.

switch places. And as the first trip was completed and that group was flying home, the next two teams were flying into Romania. What was really amazing was that even though we were taking a lot more people with us, we still had to turn away applicants!

This trip became a part of our ministry and our church. We obviously discovered some things that worked very well for college-age people, and here are the things we learned:

1. Have an Aspect of Exposure

Many people, especially in America, have huge misperceptions of what it means to be a missionary. Our students saw people with four-year degrees volunteering in the nursery to hold, change, and feed babies. They saw a guy from Sweden help with the computers. They saw some Germans teach orphans the construction trade, and people from Switzerland taught the kids to be mechanics. They were exposed to just about every vocation in one way or another, and they saw how any trade can be used on the mission field. Suddenly these students saw how their own fields of interest could potentially be used for the benefit of someone else, rather than just for themselves. That's not to say they had to move to Romania to use their vocations for God, but it helped them to think through their vocations very differently. This was one of the biggest long-term impacts of our trips. Far too many people feel as though they have to abandon a particular field of ministry in order to "do something for God." That couldn't be more false.

I've also led some trips to Cambodia, India, and Vietnam where we limited the serving aspect and focused almost solely on exposure. These trips were designed to expose college-age people to as many different types of missionary work as possible. They saw all kinds of things from a music teacher volunteering in a Cambodian orphanage to a guy who started a church and seminary in India. They saw a mechanic training orphans in that trade, a second-grade teacher on a mission base, or a stay-at-home mom. The goal was to get those who went on the trip to think through their vocational perspectives and life direction differently. And by exposing them to all kinds of people, trades, and stories, their perspective was easily changed. Even if they don't move overseas, this is a life lesson we can teach: You don't have to abandon a profession to live your life for God.

2. Give the Opportunity to Serve

Giving people an opportunity to give of themselves during a trip is huge. For us, putting on the kids' camps in Romania wasn't just physically draining, but also emotionally draining. Having people come back exhausted yet fulfilled is a great outcome for these trips, so planning in light of that is good. In addition, the service aspect allows college-age people (or anyone, for that matter) to plan, organize, be creative (with crafts, games, and so on), and implement all kinds of things. They can be a part of bringing a solution and accomplishing something that brings a sense of justice to a situation.

3. Plan for the Building of Relationships

Being able to be with the same people for a week in Romania—ministering to them, sleeping and eating by them—was a huge benefit to the long-term impact for not only those who went, but also those we ministered to. College-age people are relationally driven, so getting to know these orphans was one of the most powerful—and heartbreaking—experiences we had. Planning trips that allow relationships to develop can be a major factor to keep in mind if we want a trip with lasting impact.

The relational aspect doesn't have to be with hurting people, but it could be with a missionary who shows your team around. Whatever the case, it's very helpful to intentionally build in time for relationships. It can be as simple as planning for each group to stay with the same driver all week long. It's just a matter of spending time with the same people.

In mission trips with college-age people, I highly recommend that you make sure these three aspects—exposure, service, and relationships—are at the core of every part of every trip you do.

ADJUST AS YOU LEARN

Not everything went perfectly for us, of course. Even in some of the good things that happened on this first trip, there were surprises. For instance the fact that we had three people who immediately planned to move there (one moved a couple of years later) was great. But there were some real issues that came along with that, which I hadn't anticipated. As much as we tried to prepare the people before they moved, we didn't allow enough time. In fact one girl moved back to the States after being in Romania only a short time. It's easy to be excited about their steps of faith, and you certainly don't want to rob them of their enthusiasm in any way. But as leaders we have a responsibility to walk alongside people beyond the actual mission trip—especially those who feel committed to giving more of their lives to the cause. We must encourage and challenge them as they prepare to go long term.

Differentiating between feeling and calling isn't an easy thing to do—especially when the person is so passionate about what she's doing and has developed a heart for the people. In our case, it was necessary for the young woman to move back after a few months, but it caused some damage to the ministry in Romania. The last thing the orphans needed was for someone to come into their lives—who they believed was going to be there for the long haul—and then leave. It required a ton of energy from the leaders in that ministry to minimize the long-term damage for the kids. This particular situation forced me to put some very strict boundaries on our future trips.

The biggest change was that, prior to future trips, we let people know that if they felt a desire to go back and serve in that location long term, then they'd have to go through a six-month process with our missions pastor (or team) beforehand. During this waiting period they'd do more cultural investigation, meet with other missionaries, take some theology classes, and so on. This process wasn't put in place to rob people of their faith but to help them discern between emotional decisions and steps being taken out of true obedience to God. And those who went through the process were healthier because of it. Our heart was simply to protect both the people in our ministry, as well as the ministries overseas. Going for a short amount of time and having everyone know it's for a short time is one thing. But if someone moves there and then ends up staying for only a short time, it can cause major damage.

The point was to do our best to prepare them for the long term, and we found that giving it a time period really helped. For some college-age people becoming a missionary can just be a great and noble excuse to avoid facing obstacles and pressures here at home. It's attractive because it's new, exciting, and offers some kind of direction for their lives. I've found this happens more frequently than I'd like to admit. This has to be watched with college-age people.

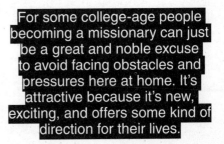

For some college-age people becoming a missionary can just be a great and noble excuse to avoid facing obstacles and pressures here at home. It's attractive because it's new, exciting, and offers some kind of direction for their lives.

We learned that although having a relational aspect in the trip is necessary, there are things we need to be watchful of. People are emotional on these trips anyway, and when you add relational connections to that emotion, it can be dangerous. Their hearts go out to people when they hear their stories. They fall in love with the kids and people. And although God can use these trips to move college-age people halfway across the world to serve him, God could also just be using that time to help young adults be more faithful *wherever* they currently live. We need to be open to both possibilities and ready to guide either one.

TEACHABLE MOMENTS

If you take a trip to a second-world country like Romania or a third-world country like India or Cambodia, expect the college-age people on your mission team to be rocked. Expect their hearts to be engaged and their minds to do some intellectual gymnastics. Be prepared to deal with the anger they may feel toward Americans and the American lifestyle when they return home. They usually view the amount of money, how it's used, and the overabundance of material possessions as repulsive after these experiences—and, in many ways, rightly so. But how they handle those feelings can be another story. As leaders we have a chance to seize, as well as create, teachable moments to help people process the trip in an effective way.

I remember a trip we took to India. We served in a few ways there, but the trip was more of an exposure trip. We went to two or three different ministries a day and listened to the stories of the missionaries who served there. We spent 12 days in the slums of India, where the poorest of the poor live. We were in some tribal areas outside of Mumbai (what we refer to as Bombay), as well as some slum areas in the city. In fact Mumbai is said to have the largest slum area in all of Asia having more than 1 million people living in this one slum. It's unbelievable to spend time there. Heartbreaking, for sure.

One purpose of the exposure trip is to expose people not just to missionary possibilities, but also to the culture. So I did something a bit risky at the end of the trip. I didn't tell anyone what we were going to do; but on the very last day, we packed up in our rural location and headed into the city for our last night. Nobody knew where we were going. We took the train into the city (which is a total experience in itself!), and then we took a cab from the train station to the Gateway of India. (It's a national landmark that you may have seen in pictures.) We gathered there, sat down by the water, and debriefed some of the trip. Being right next to the slum area, we talked about our time there, the things we saw, the things that stood out to us, and those that broke our hearts. When we were done I told everyone to put on their backpacks because we were going to walk to where we'd be staying for the night.

They didn't realize it at the time, but we were already there. Directly across the street from where we were sitting was the Taj Mahal Hotel. It's five stars plus, and it's the nicest place I've ever stayed—anywhere. For instance if you go to the pool, a personal servant waits on you. If you want anything, this person gets it for you.

People were shocked.

No, actually they were angry.

"How could we go through all of this, learn what we did during the past two weeks, and then stay *here* tonight?" they asked. "How much are we paying for this?" another person asked as he pulled me aside.

The intellectual gymnastics began.

I told everyone to go to their rooms, take a shower, and meet back in the lobby in an hour. After that hour we walked down the street to a restaurant to get dinner and discuss the issue. There were some real times of tension; but in the end, it was a great teachable moment. The bottom line was that right outside the walls of this amazing hotel was the largest slum in all of Asia. But India has both extremes, and I wanted them to see that. In addition, I didn't want them to just understand it in theory—I wanted them to *feel* the dichotomy between the two worlds. And they definitely felt it. It was a challenge for them to begin thinking about what they valued as they went back home. We talked about the abundance of comfort we live in every day and how when we go back home we have a choice: We can remember the stark contrast we live in compared to the rest of the world, or we can go through life focused on our own comfort and forgetting how others live.

KEEPING THE GOAL IN MIND

Designing mission trips that have a balance of exposure, service, and relationships is what makes them effective with college-age people. Being intentional about planning teachable moments adds to the impact. But in the midst of all this, we can't forget about our goal of assimilating college-age people into our church as a whole. We have to make sure every aspect of our ministries works toward this end, and mission trips are no exception.

So I've found three specific things to be very helpful:

1. Invite Older Believers on the Trip

This is a pretty obvious idea, but it's a phenomenal way to have mission trips feed our end goal of deeper intergenerational connection. We've had older adults come along and shoot video, be a part of a team, and even lead a team. The key is simply having them join us. When a college-age person and an older adult share this type of experience, remaining connected back home is much easier.

2. Go Where Your Church Has Already Developed Relationships

One of the things I didn't think about until some years after we'd started taking these trips was going to places where our church already had connections. If your church has supported a particular missionary for a long time and you believe that particular ministry will have exposure, service, and relational aspects to it, then go there. When the college-age people get to know these missionaries and hear about how much their relationship with your church has meant to them over time, it allows them to feel a part of the church as a whole. I've seen college-age people come into these existing relationships and further the missionaries' connection with the church. Those college-age people who naturally connect with the missionary, or others in the ministry, will automatically feel more connected to your church.

3. Encourage Older Believers to Continue Relationships After the Trip

After the mission trip ends, older adults should be prodded to spend time with those college-age people they became closest with on the trip. The connection was naturally made, so now it's just a matter of continuing it. Another practical thing we can encourage older adults to do is share about their mission trip experience with all of their friends. The more honest they are about what they learned and, in particular, how much they value the relationships they built with college-age people over the course of the trip, the better.

We have to make sure every aspect of our ministries works toward our goal of assimilating college-age people into our church as a whole, and mission trips are no exception.

THE BOTTOM LINE

- Three key aspects should be emphasized on mission trips: Exposure, service, and relationships.

- We need to protect the hearts of zealous and passionate college-age people.

- Intentionally plan teachable moments that force deeper thought processes.

- Mission trips can be a vehicle for assimilation.

NOTES:

Many college ministries have retreats and other events throughout the year. Some do them only in winter, some include summer trips, while others do one a season. How you approach doing retreats with your college-age people will depend on your context, but I believe that doing something regularly is universally needed. Getting people away from their normal routines can accomplish so many things, especially if we're intentional in a few specific areas.

I remember the very first trip we did in our college ministry. I waited for a while before doing anything because I wanted to make sure that what we did was a good fit and would be something we could build a tradition around. We ended up joining another church that had been doing a snowboarding trip to Utah for the previous five years. We were located in Southern California, so going to Utah was an attractive and doable adventure. I still remember the nine of us driving out there in our church van. Man, that was a lot of fun. Joining with another church is a great way to begin doing trips—and I'd recommend that anyone who's just starting off consider this option.

This church already had a system for doing things. They had a relationship with a hotel, had a plan for meals, and knew the resort we were going to every day. This was perfect for me, since I was just beginning. The other college pastor and I shared the teaching time, and it worked out great.

> Getting people away from their normal routines provides the setting for developing meaningful peer relationships as well as deeper connections to the church as a whole.

This winter trip became a huge success—so much so, that we made it a tradition. Some things, like vehicles and location, changed as the numbers grew. On one trip we took 270 college-age people in six buses. And oh man, talk about a nightmare! Keeping six bus drivers who don't know each other together for a 15-hour drive will give Tylenol a headache. But despite the logistics, we always had a ton of fun playing games, laughing, getting into deep conversations, watching movies, and so on. Even the bus ride became an important part of the trip and vital for developing relationships.

Trips like this can be a logistical nightmare, but they can be a great part of our ministries, too. This annual trip of ours proved to be effective in attracting new people, and a lot of good came out of it. Through trial and error we stumbled upon some things that worked very well with college-age people.

THINGS THAT WORK

From one year to the next, we tweaked how we did things. But no matter where we went or what we did, there were universal things we found to be effective with college-age retreats.

1. Do a Few and Do Them Well

I'm a firm believer in doing a few things and doing those things well. Trying to do too many events will inevitably cause all of them to lose their impact. Pick a couple of things you do annually and make these *the* trips.

2. Keep the Cost Down

College-age people don't usually have a ton of extra money lying around, yet everything has a cost. But there are some things that can help. For instance we offered different packages: A base package included transportation, lodging, meals, and some activities; another package included a one-day lift ticket, while another package included lift tickets for two days, and a third package offered three-day lift tickets. The base amount was pretty low, which allowed people who couldn't afford much to still be a part of the trip. There are all kinds of things you can do to keep the cost down, but offering different packages is a great and simple way to do it.

You can also:

- Plan your trip during weekdays, if at all possible. We did our Utah trip during winter break, so this worked for us. It saved a lot of money on hotel rooms, and it really kept the overall costs down.

- Ask the hotel about complimentary rooms for leaders. Most of the time they'll give you free rooms—usually suites.

- Offer payment plans. As soon as we started promoting the trip, we let people know that we could place them on a payment plan. Of course this took some administrative work, but working out a monthly payment plan can be a great help. Some people, unfortunately, didn't end up paying their full amount. But this allowed for a lot of teachable moments, too—which were priceless. Here are a few recommendations for this payment approach: (1) Offer them only for the base amount, not things like lift tickets or other extras, (2) Have a minimum amount that they have to pay before they can go on the trip—at least the cost of the deposit, and (3) Develop a very short contract between the church and the student that details the payment due dates and amounts.

- Do fundraisers. If your church allows this, these can of course help.

- Seek sponsors. If there are older adults in your church who are already involved with college-age people, consider asking them to sponsor a student or three. You can divide these amounts any way you want, but having people donate toward this cause can really help.

- Be wise. It isn't necessary to spend money on some things—like fliers. With all the technology that we have available today, we can invite people—even have sign-ups—in ways that don't cost money. Flyers aren't the issue; the issue is thinking through ways we can do things that don't cost money. These small costs add up over time, and many of them aren't even *necessary*.

- Shop around. If you're checking out places to stay, make sure those places know that you're also seeking pricing from others. If you find a better deal at one place, go back to the other and let them know what they offered you. You might be surprised at how flexible they become.

3. Eat Well

I'm not saying be extravagant in this area, but make sure you provide at least one good meal a day. It doesn't matter if you cook it yourself or have it catered, but having one really good meal, like dinner, all together can make all the difference in the world. On our Utah trip we had dinner together each night catered by the hotel. After a long day on the slopes, people were able to come back to a nice room, sit down with eight or so other people, and have a catered meal. For college-age people this is a great thing, and it doesn't cost much more—especially if you're already staying in the hotel. Believe me, it's worth the extra $3 a meal.

We also provided a sort of continental breakfast for everyone (I'll explain this in more detail in the next section), and they were on their own for lunch. Logistically this worked better since everyone was scattered around the ski lodge over the course of the day. Providing two meals a day, versus three, also helped to keep the overall cost down.

4. Stay at a Decent Place

Don't go for the cheapest hotel in the area. Again, I'm not suggesting you stay at a five-star hotel, but it should be a nice place. You can always negotiate with the hotel sales people on prices; and the more people you bring, the more you can talk them down. Plus, when you put four people in a room, the price per person isn't that much—especially with a group discount.

A tip: If you're staying at a hotel, make sure you put a place on the registration form for people to request a roommate. They'll likely be sharing a bed with someone, so make sure they have at least one person they know well staying in their hotel room. For those who may feel uncomfortable about sharing a room with others (especially guys), a nice hotel helps them see past that.

Some things you want to look for in a hotel are—

- A room to meet in—and possibly other rooms to utilize for night options

- A nice lobby that's conducive for hanging out

- A hotel staff that doesn't mind if people are playing board games until midnight or later

- A pool or hot tub—for winter retreats, having an indoor hot tub is a great attraction. (Of course, encouraging retreat-goers to wear modest swimwear is beneficial.) Plus, we even used the hot tub for a baptismal at times.

- A good location—the closer you stay to things like a mall, movie theater, or restaurants, the better. And it should have a bus stop nearby so people can get around on their own. For trips like our winter retreat, where some people don't purchase lift tickets, there should be other things for them to do. So location is key.

If you have the opportunity to stay in a nice house or cabin, this can be a great option as well. Having everyone in one location for everything can help keep the costs down. But with everyone all together, it's even more important to make sure that it's nice, comfortable, and has what everyone needs.

5. Have Little Surprises

It's great to start off with a bang. On our Utah trip, we used to bring in fresh, hot Krispy Kreme doughnuts immediately following our first night meeting. On other nights you can do very inexpensive things like provide popcorn while watching a movie. Beyond this I also sought sponsors who might want to give away things as a promotion for their companies. For our Utah trip I simply went around to local sporting goods stores, skate shops, and so on and let them know we were doing a trip with college-age people. I asked if they had anything we could hand out to the people during our meetings. We got everything from stickers to hand warmers to snowboards. It's crazy how easy it was when I took just a few minutes and personally asked the owners. Anyway, having some very small things like this to give away in meeting times or on the bus can go a long way.

6. Provide Information

When the buses pulled up to the hotel in Utah, we had registration ready to go. People walked in and got their room keys, a schedule for the week, and other pertinent details. Having a schedule printed on a half sheet of paper or the back of laminated nametags to be worn around their necks isn't expensive. We also provided bus schedules to the resort, city bus charts, times that certain shops or restaurants were open in the area, movie times, and even a listing of entertainment options. Making this short and concise is best. In other words don't overwhelm them with a book but provide clear information so you limit the amount of ongoing information that needs to be relayed during your meeting times.

7. Give Freedom

It's important to trust people. These are college-age people, not junior high students. They have freedoms in everyday life that you don't want to impede. For instance they don't have a bedtime at home, so don't give them one on the trip. They live with some standards, but their parents probably don't ask them where they're going every time they leave the house. It's important to watch the amount of things we *require* of them.

For example the only things we asked people to attend were the dinner and the evening meeting. That was it. They had a schedule for the next day, so they knew what was available and could do whatever they wished. Buses left for the resort at different times, so if they wanted to sleep in—they did so. If they wanted to wake up early and be the first one on the lift, then they could do that, too. Freedom is very important on these retreats. At the end of the night meeting, I'd announce some night options that were available to them and then I'd simply say, "We'll see you tomorrow night at dinner, if not before!"

8. Minimize and Maximize Meetings

Many times we feel as though we need to fill the schedule with a ton of meetings and seminars to make the retreat worthwhile. I couldn't disagree more! Of course there might be certain retreats you plan for a certain type of people that can be designed around meetings. But if it's open to everyone, then you want to avoid this tendency at all costs. My recommendation is to minimize the amount of meetings but maximize what you do in them. I'm not saying make them long and do a bunch of different things. I'm talking about making them meaningful, in-depth, and worshipful. Do a few meetings and do them well.

Again, using our Utah trip as an example, we had only one meeting a day. It was after dinner, and it was about 90 minutes long. We had a worship band, and we had someone teach on a theme. We wanted those in attendance to think through one thing all weekend, process it with others, and consider how they might embrace that idea in their lives. That was it. We minimized the amount of meetings, but we sought to maximize the impact by concentrating on one theme. The last thing you want to do is exhaust their time by giving them a bunch of information. Give them some, but make sure they have time and space to process what you give them. Most people don't drink from a fire hose. Drinking from water fountains works much better.

9. Provide Options

This stems off the previous tip. We provided a wide variety of late-night options that people could do. We showed movies, we had a room filled with board games, we put on different types of tournaments, we had optional worship times, and we even offered discussion groups based on the retreat theme. Planning and offering multiple choices like this is great, but make sure they're optional. What you'll find is that most of them will be utilized to some degree, but you'll also see people just hanging out and talking in a hotel hallway. And all of these things are good.

KEEPING THE BIG PICTURE IN MIND

There is a lot of value in getting college-age people away, by themselves. The atmosphere is conducive for hitting core age-stage issues, and it can be a great time of connecting with their peers. On the other hand we can really use these times to help them have a deeper connection with the larger church body. This is crucial in college-age ministry, and retreats can be one of the best ways to accomplish this.

Here are some things you can do to help this connection happen naturally:

- Pick one couple for every 25 college-age people and ask them to come on your trip. Their job is *not* to chaperone; it's just to hang out. You have to handpick this couple! Their ages don't matter, but there are some basic characteristics that you want this couple to have: Solid in their faith, honest and willing to speak their minds, fun, relaxed, and willing to hang out late at night playing cards, board games, and so on.

- Have the couple(s) host breakfast. Buy some breakfast food (cereal, fruit, bagels, and so on), give the couple a suite in the hotel or a designated area just for them, and have them host a breakfast gathering each morning for those attending the retreat. The couple will simply set out the food, and the college-age people can go to the couple's suite to eat and hang out. Some will come, eat, and then leave. Others will hang out for a long time just talking. The couple has to be relaxed during this time . . . just hanging out, laughing, and eating.

- Don't give the couple *any* other tasks. Their only job is to hang out and be available. If they ski or snowboard, let them go all day. If they don't, then encourage them to go to the lodge and hang out around lunchtime, have lunch with people who stay behind, or cruise around the mall with someone they clicked with. Remember, the goal is relational connection, so make sure they have time and space to build relationships. If you need an extra pair of hands during the retreat, ask those college-age people who needed scholarships to help with the details, rather than utilizing the adults. These are friends of yours, and they are there to hang out. It's important that you set them up as "normal" people, not chaperones or staff.

- Pray for natural connections to happen. I've found that when we expose college-age people to older, mature believers in these ways, natural mentoring relationships form. We don't need to overstructure it; we just need to pray. Set aside some times where you pray for the relationships and connections. Frequently check in with the adults you bring along and ask them if they're getting to know some people. Typically if they're just hanging out anyway and are simply available, you don't even need to ask them because it will be obvious.

Winter retreats can be fun no matter what, but we can also be very intentional with making them a part of our goal of assimilation. It's not rocket science—just do a few things, keep it simple, and watch things happen.

It's not rocket science—just do a few things, keep it simple, and watch things happen.

SOME QUICK TIPS FOR LEADING COLLEGE-AGE RETREATS

- Let students lead various aspects of the trip. Leaders in your ministry will naturally take on things, but make sure to use this as an opportunity for others to step up and take on responsibilities as well.

- Choose an age range for the trip (like 18 to 25), make it clear, and make no exceptions. Think through how you'll address those who are outside of this age range. There can be some sticky situations, so make sure you think through your reasoning for the range you give.

- Have a theme and use that theme in as many aspects of the trip as possible (shirts, messages or studies, decor, and so on). Have one thing you want people to embrace and then make sure that one thing intermingles in between everything else.

- Do activities that everyone can participate in.

- Make sure any promotional material is clear and precise. For instance if the fee doesn't cover the cost for all of the meals, specify which ones it will cover and what they should expect to do for the others.

- Utilize Internet-based advertising. This can save you a lot of money. Having fliers can be beneficial, but maximize the tools that are available at no cost.

- If you've never done a trip before, use preregistration as a tool to get an idea of how many people will attend. Have them make a nonrefundable deposit by a certain date. It doesn't have to be much, but this can give you an idea of how many people to expect. But be prepared for anything.

- Be careful with "mixers." I'm not saying don't do them, but for some people these can be very uncomfortable and feel forced. On retreats we don't need to push relationships; they'll happen naturally.

- When it's time to clean up, make sure you do the bulk of it at a time when the most people can pitch in and help. For instance have all the cleanup take place right before the last meal or meeting.

THE BOTTOM LINE

- Retreats need to be simple, done well, inexpensive, and focused on age-stage issues.

- Retreats can be a great catalyst for helping our long-term goal of assimilation.

NOTES:

CHAPTER 16

WORKING WITH INTERNS

Scott attended a college about 20 minutes from our church. He started coming to church with some friends and his girlfriend at the time, Lara.[31] As I got to know Scott, over dozens of cups of coffee and lunches, I began to see a ton of potential in him. He was sharp, he genuinely desired to honor God in every aspect of his life, and he wanted to be in vocational ministry. At one point he asked if I'd spend more intentional time with him because he wanted to be exposed to what ministry was like. I'd grown to love him, and he had the character and potential—so that was a no-brainer.

When people ask this question, they're usually thinking about things like what we *do* in ministry, what an average week looks like, how we manage our time, or how the inner workings of a church office work.

This is very normal, but I never start there.

Before anything else I want people to understand the *heart* behind what we do.

So rather than have Scott shadow me through my days or spend time with other staff members, we studied 1 Thessalonians together. We pretty much followed the pattern I set out for you in chapter 11 (Scott read a section, wrote down any questions or thoughts, and then we talked through the passage together). I chose 1 Thessalonians because I love Paul's perspective for the people in this church. I wanted Scott to see Paul's heart for them and to notice aspects of Paul's—for lack of a better term—leadership style.

There were some very specific things I wanted Scott to see, such as—

- Paul shared not only the gospel with these people, but also his life (2:3, 8).

---

31. Their names have been changed to protect their privacy.

- Paul sought to please *only* God (2:4-6).

- Paul deeply loved people, being gentle like a mother with a newborn (2:7-8).

- Paul sought to serve people (2:9).

- Paul was godly and exhorted people to follow his example (2:10-12; 4:1-12).

- Paul was uniquely concerned about the people's *faith* (1:8; 3:1-10).

- Paul prayed for the people constantly (3:10-13).

I didn't tell Scott these things in the beginning; I wanted him to see them for himself. So my direction was simple. I told him to make sure he paid attention to Paul's perspective and heart for the people and what he seems to be concerned about in their lives. I could have listed much more than I did above, but these are the types of things I wanted Scott to see and embrace before he began thinking through what I *do* on a daily basis. Learning what needs to be done is a part of things, but understanding the heart of a spiritual leader is much more important.

Spiritual leadership isn't about doing events. Anyone can do that.

Being a spiritual leader, vocational or not, requires us to understand how God uses who he's made us to be in the lives of people. I could show Scott all the ins and outs of the day-to-day things, but if he didn't understand this concept, then he'd never last in ministry.

When we're investing in people for ministry, we need to make sure we cultivate the right heart and perspective in them for what they'll be doing. Instead, we tend to jump straight into delegating tasks, assigning roles, showing them how to develop a calendar of events, and working on their teaching and organizational skills.

I believe that's a very dangerous place to start.

When we're investing in people for ministry, we need to make sure we cultivate the right heart and perspective in them for what they'll be doing.

To help cultivate the right heart and perspective with Scott, we not only looked at Paul's letters to the Thessalonians, but also spent time on Paul's letters to

Timothy and Titus. Once we finished that, I moved on to show him other things. Well, actually, I take that back.

INTERNSHIPS ARE ABOUT DISCOVERY

Eventually I hired Scott as an intern, but I have a little different approach to working with interns than others do. You certainly don't have to agree with me on this, and I'm not saying this is the only or the best way. But I'd like to explain what I do and a little bit about why.

On Scott's first day I gave him one ongoing task to oversee: The setup and teardown of our Sunday night ministry. It was a decent-sized task, and keeping a team of people motivated for this wasn't the easiest thing in the world. But this was a maximum of five hours of work a week, and he was required to work 20 to 25 hours a week. Then I gave him some, admittedly ambiguous, direction for the remaining 15 to 20 hours a week: "Think through where the needs are in the ministry and how you fit into those." This is the first thing he'd need to do if he was hired at another church, so I figured giving him the experience right away in an internship is great preparation.

Part of an internship is discovering things about yourself. I didn't want Scott to jump straight into doing things. I wanted him to discover how God uniquely made him and how God could use him in the lives of other people in our ministry. Therefore I didn't want to fill his time with a bunch of tasks. I wanted him to have space to discover how he could be used in people's lives. So minimizing the amount of tasks forced him to spend time with people. He certainly didn't have anything else to do with his time!

I believe in hiring people for who they are, not necessarily what they do. I encouraged Scott to think through the following questions as he met with people: *How might God use who he's made me to be in our church? What strengths do I have that are needed here? In what ways does God seem to be using me in the lives of other people?*

Scott would come into my office from time to time, frustrated by the lack of direction I gave him. He was always very respectful, but he felt like he was being a poor steward of the church's money by not "doing" enough. I'd listen to him, but I'd always respond with something like, "I told you what I want you to do. Figure out how God wants to use who he's made you to be in the lives of other people."

Okay, maybe I'm a little mean. But I really want interns to think beyond tasks. And sometimes the only way to do this is by not assigning them. Starting off with this focus did a couple of things for Scott. Things like…wait…hold on. Before I write what this exercise accomplished, I'm going to call Scott and ask what he'd say…

Okay, I just got off the phone with Scott. (And, in case you're wondering, I *did* actually call him.) We talked for about 25 minutes, and here's what *he* said. First, this time and space made him realize that ministry is about people, and it helped him to keep that focus. He said that *before* this experience, he could have said that ministry is about people in theory; but this internship really cemented it in his mind. Second, he said it helped him to see how important his "walk with the Lord is" in ministry and how important his character was for ministry with people. He planted a church about four years ago, and he said this has really stuck with him over the years. Third, he said it really forced him to figure out how to use the overflow of what God had already done in his life to benefit others. As a pastor of a church, this is critical. I cannot emphasize the importance of this enough.

The bottom line for me was that this process forced Scott to think through who he was, and it put a very strong emphasis on his character. For me, that's success! People can have all the gifts and talents in the world, but if they don't understand who they are, have God's focus on people, and have the necessary character, then none of that would matter. Gifts and skills get people places, but character keeps them there.

Too often internships are overly focused on tasks, and I think that's a huge mistake. I know a lot of things need to be done and it can become overwhelming. While interns can help alleviate some of that pressure, there has to be more to an internship than relieving leaders of tasks they don't want to do.

I could have done a study on this with Scott, or I could have had him read a book about it. But having him figure things out on his own is what really made it stick with him over time. And it was well worth the "church's money" to invest in him in this manner.

Now, I know this approach might not work for everyone, and my point isn't to recommend this approach. I'm simply trying to get across that the principle of internships should be about discovery of self, discovery of what our focus is (people), and discovery of how God uses who he's made us to be (character) in the lives of others.

If people get hired at a church, they ought to understand the importance of these things because one day they'll have to go into another church, assess it, and then determine what to do based on who they are. Internships can be a great preparation for this.

INTERNSHIPS ARE ABOUT EXPOSURE

Having said all that, internships are also about exposing people to different aspects of ministry, and daily tasks are a piece of that. Interns need to try different things and even be forced to do things they're obviously not good at doing. Through a variety of exposures, they'll see what comes naturally to them, what they struggle with, and what they like or don't like to do.

It wasn't hard to see that Scott was organized and extremely gifted with administrative things. I remember putting him in charge of overseeing a concession stand for a massive festival that our church was doing. The amount of food and volunteers to pull this off required him to be extremely organized. He not only had to recruit and organize the 30 or so volunteers, but he also had to figure out how to cook everything in a timely manner and develop a system for the thousands of people who'd be eating. But perhaps the most challenging thing was figuring out how much of everything to buy.

I remember checking in with Scott to see how things were going one day. I walked into the intern office, and he showed me spreadsheets with every imaginable possibility listed out. He had price breakdowns of every item, and he'd even thought through different ratios for each food item (like how many people he thought would *actually* put tomatoes on their sandwiches). It wasn't difficult to see his strength in organization and thinking. The average person doesn't try to figure out how many people would *actually* eat tomatoes!

Regardless, it was through this experience that he realized he was good at these types of things, and it really showed his ability to think ahead. Because Scott was so strong in these aspects, throughout his internship he led mission trips and small groups, and helped plan and organize retreats. There were times when I'd give him a concept to help me think through, and he'd do far better than I could have done. Putting people in positions to use their strengths is great, but it can't stop there.

Internships are about developing people as a whole—working through their weaknesses as much as developing their strengths. This is a lot of work, but it's time we have to spend if we're going to be faithful with our interns.

When you're working with interns, allow them to work in the areas they're good at, but don't let them bail on those that they're not. Like most of us, college-age people tend to want to use their gifts and do the things they're good at doing. They can even get frustrated if we push them in other areas, but it's through that challenge that they truly discover more about their strengths and learn where they'll need to ask for help.

Another kind of exposure our interns need is exposure to us, personally. And this is, perhaps, the most important kind. We need to allow interns into every aspect of our lives. They should see how we balance life with our families and ministry, go on hospital visits with us and see how we deal with those situations, and even see how we balance our checking accounts. Interns, regardless of the field they're in, usually appreciate any amount of time they can spend with leaders who are doing what they're looking to do. Exposing them to our lives, and potentially the lives of others we know in ministry, is one of the most impacting things we can do for them.

> Internships are about developing people as a whole—working through their weaknesses as much as developing their strengths.

INTERNSHIPS ARE ABOUT FORMULATING A PHILOSOPHY

If you've been in ministry for a while now, you probably have a way of doing things and reasons for why you do them that way. Maybe it works best with your personality or is the most effective for the context you're in. There are all kinds of approaches or models for ministry, and it doesn't really matter which one your church identifies with. What does matter is that you understand that approach. Successful leaders know what they do, how they approach doing those things, and can explain why that approach is best for them.

If internships are about developing leaders, then helping them formulate a philosophy of ministry is vital. If people finish an internship with us and cannot explain what we do, how we do those things, and why we take that approach, then we haven't done our job. Furthermore, if we don't help them articulate how they might differ from our approach, then we haven't prepared them the way we ought to.

Throughout my years of helping interns formulate a philosophy of ministry, one thing I've done is to have them constantly rework our existing one. To do this, talk your intern through what you're currently doing in a particular area and then ask him or her to rethink that approach. Ask the intern to critique it. This not only challenges the intern, but it's a healthy way for us as leaders to avoid getting stuck in a rut of ministry. Talk about the philosophy differences, brainstorm, and even disagree. It may be helpful to have them articulate their views on paper. The goal is not to get an intern to agree with you but to force them to think through ministry for themselves.

Internships are a way of investing in people, helping them discover who they are and how they work best, and then developing an approach to ministry that fits them. Those who've interned under me haven't agreed with everything I've done. During my phone conversation with Scott, I asked him how he approaches things differently with his interns from the way I did with him. He told me a couple of things he does that work better for him. I think this is wonderful. He knows what works for him, and he has reasons for it. I love the fact that God used me to play a small part in that process for Scott—and that I can learn from him now!

INTERNSHIPS ARE ABOUT DEVELOPING PEOPLE

Tracking progress is key to any type of development, and internships are no exception. Internships are about a wide variety of things: Helping people understand the heart of a spiritual leader, their own identities, and the importance of character; developing giftedness; helping them in their weak areas; and developing a philosophy of ministry. Evaluating the progress of each of these areas is important. This evaluation process shouldn't be awkward or overly formal, but having a way to measure the progress of each intern is important.

Over the years I've developed the following list of things to evaluate interns. I'll usually rate them from one to five in each area, with five representing a readiness to lead a ministry in that area:

- *Reliability on Scripture.* Evaluate how well the intern's thoughts and actions are driven by Scripture. Make sure the intern is developing convictions for his or her life and ministry from a personal study of

Scripture, and that the intern has a good balance between growing in his or her personal faith and working in ministry.

- *Teachability.* Evaluate how the person takes constructive criticism from pastors as well as peers and how she cooperates when direction is provided—especially when she disagrees or doesn't want to do it.

- *Discipleship.* Evaluate the intern's skills as he or she disciples the people in your ministry and how the intern speaks into the lives of volunteers or, if applicable, other staff members.

- *Teamwork.* This is an evaluation of how the person works within a ministry team. Is the intern divisive and controlling? Does he or she contribute and constructively disagree? Also evaluate how well the intern understands the overall mission of the church and if he or she is working within those parameters.

- *Administration.* Evaluate how well the person balances his or her personal schedule, prioritizes daily life and tasks, and communicates with the leader, volunteers, and other staff members when needed.

- *Personal Character.* Choose some specific characteristics to evaluate, such as overall humility, honesty, compassion for others, and desire for godliness.

- *Quantity of Work.* This is an evaluation of the volume of work the person accomplishes. Everyone has a different capacity in this area, so helping people understand where their limits—or laziness—are is an important part of the evaluation. College-age people generally aren't known for their discipline. They often talk about how much they're working, and although there can be truth to this, often they just don't use their time efficiently. So evaluating an intern on this is very important and can provide some fruitful teachable moments.

- *Quality of Work.* Evaluate overall judgment in decision making, organization, and thoroughness.

- *Creativity.* Evaluate whether or not the person can develop, articulate, and implement a vision. This can be in large or small things, but the evaluation is on the intern's ideas and whether or not he or she can implement them effectively.

- *Dependability.* Evaluate whether or not the person can be depended on. This of course needs to be within the limits of the intern's experience and training, but helping someone understand where he or she is with this is vital to the person's development.

- *Leadership.* This may be the toughest one to gauge. People have different ways of leading people—some are great with smaller groups, while others work much better with larger ones. There are all kinds of variances, but the bottom line here is whether or not other people respect, are drawn to, and follow this person.

TIME WELL SPENT

I want to end here by recommending that you be very careful about who you choose as an intern. The reality is that having an intern takes a great deal of your time. You're essentially going to disciple this person in every aspect of life, and this always takes more time than expected. I have a friend and mentor who says, "Remember, *disciple* is spelled T-I-M-E."

In addition it's important to realize that the time you spend with this person will be taking time away from other things. So be careful about in whom you choose to invest such a large amount of time. I personally look for people who are passionate (you can't teach that), who fully embrace the mission of the church, who've already been serving for a while, who have a sense of calling to and show signs of giftedness in vocational ministry, and who are humble and eager to learn. It's important to be willing to spend time with anyone, but be careful in choosing who you'll invest in on a deeper level.

Remember, *disciple* is spelled T-I-M-E.

THE BOTTOM LINE

- Internships are more about developing people for their future lives in ministry than relieving us of undesirable tasks today.

- The development and processes of our interns ought to be measured and evaluated.

NOTES:

CHAPTER 17

CHURCH-BASED CAMPUS MINISTRY

....

Throughout this book I haven't focused much on reaching out to those outside our immediate church context. This isn't because I don't believe it's important. Quite the contrary. Campuses are a mission field that our ministries *must* focus on. Not doing so is like a high school ministry not paying any attention to the area high schools. It doesn't make any sense.

Resources, including time, might be an issue for you. Figuring out how to get on campus and knowing where to start can be tough. Challenges like these are why I wrote this chapter.[32]

I am a firm believer that the best way to reach campuses, especially commuter schools, is by investing in those who are currently a part of our ministries. In other words, college-age people are most effective with college-age people. I hope I've made it clear that peer relationships aren't the end we're working toward, but it's a great place to start when we're seeking to reach out to people on a campus. I've also been clear that numerical growth is not *the* measure of our success, but this doesn't mean we shouldn't pursue having a greater impact. And I'd even suggest that if those in our ministry aren't reaching out to others, at least to some degree, then we're not doing our job as spiritual leaders.

> Campuses are a mission field that our ministries *must* focus on.

But what do we do? Should we go on the campus and just hang out? Do we figure out a campaign strategy to implement on campus?

Sifting through these types of questions and trying to figure out where to start can be daunting. This chapter contains some of the things I've seen that have long-term impact for reaching people on a campus. But first I want to issue a disclaimer: Every campus has a different culture, traditions,

---

32. If you're interested in reading more on reaching campuses, check out Benson Hines' free e-book called "Reaching the Campus Tribes" (http://reachingthecampustribes.com).

values, and even types of people from others around the country. So be careful. Regardless of whether you're trying to reach people on a commuter campus (few or no students living on campus) or a university in a college town (the town pretty much revolves around campus life), getting to know the uniqueness of that campus takes a significant amount of time. But the time you spend is well worth it, so take the time and get to know who you're trying to reach.

COMMUTER CAMPUSES

For the past dozen years or so, I've worked mainly with commuter schools. In Simi Valley there was a community college with 13,000 students in the next city over, and even Cal State University of Northridge (about 25 minutes away from the church I worked for) with 38,000 students had fewer than 2,000 students living on campus. Now I live in Portland where commuter schools are in the majority by far. The population of college-age people here is much greater than in Simi Valley, but commuter campuses have some very similar characteristics regardless of the location.

Most students are there strictly for class, and then they're quickly off to work. With little, if any, campus life at commuter schools, meeting people and building relationships with students can take a tremendous amount of time. Within a 20-mile radius of my home in Portland, there are four community colleges, totaling more than 75,000 students—and this doesn't include Portland State (18,000 students) or any of the private schools or trade schools. Needless to say, there is no shortage of college-age people in the area—which is one of the reasons I moved here to plant a church. But just because there is a large number of them, that doesn't make it easy to get to know them—especially on campus. Commuter campuses are tough. But there are a few things I've seen as being effective:

1. Get Close to Campus

Find the coffee shops near campus and spend time in them. If you spend enough time there, you'll inevitably, and naturally, meet people. You share electrical outlets, stand in line with them, talk with the employees, and at busy hours you might even share a table with them.

2. Invest in Students in Your Church

I happen to think the most effective thing, by far, is students reaching students. The best way to build community on a commuter campus is by impacting one student at a time. During your time with your students, spend a great deal of time cultivating a heart in them for their peers at school. Help them view their school as it is: The mission field that God has them on today.

3. Plan Events Carefully

People aren't on campus for long, and they're usually on their way to class or their cars. So initiating conversations can come across as little more than a sales pitch. And this typically just annoys people who are on their way somewhere else. Since students are typically on the go, they aren't generally interested in campus events. But if you're going to do something on campus, something service-oriented can be good. Hand out coffee and hot chocolate on cold days, or cold sodas and water on hot ones. Hand out free coffee during finals week. These types of service events can be a great way to catch the eye of students in passing. Focusing an event around lunchtime is also a good strategy because there are fewer classes, leaving more natural time for conversations to take place.

4. Take a Class

This might seem weird at first, but it can really be a great way to get to know some students on campus. Most commuter schools have a lot of older people attending anyway, so blending in with the student body is easier. Just take your time and try to meet one student at a time. Taking classes on philosophy or religion can be a great place to start. Most schools will have a class titled something like, "Man, Nature, God." These are typically discussion-oriented courses and the conversations often continue even after class is over. If you have the time, joining a class as a learner and one who simply contributes to the dialogue of the class is a great way to get a feel for the students on a particular campus.

5. Connect with Philosophy Teachers

Even if you're unable to take a class, you can still connect with teachers on campus. Many philosophy professors will have guests from different belief systems share their thoughts about a particular issue or be part of a panel discussion. Offer yourself as a resource to these professors. Approach them humbly and with an attitude of service. If you come across as arrogant or as someone who just wants to preach to people, it's unlikely you'll be invited. Make yourself available, but don't be pushy.

6. Develop a Club

Sometimes clubs can be an effective way to integrate onto a campus. Clubs can also get funding and access to rooms on campus. My personal recommendation is not to form a specifically Christian club. I know that seems backward, but these tend to have a negative stigma—at least they have on the campuses that I've worked with. But something like a club designed for social justice or community service can be effective in attracting even nonbelievers. I'd recommend having your gathering times be discussion based and a place where every opinion is valued. You don't have to abandon solid doctrine, and you can let people know it's led by Christians. But designing it as a place for dialogue is especially helpful on commuter campuses. I've found that if people can engage and share their opinions, they'll be more likely to stop by, even on their way to work.

7. Have Lunchtime Bible Studies

Consider having a time during the lunch hour where you have a very short prayer or Bible study time. This can be a way to integrate onto a campus and connect with some Christian students. Encourage them as missionaries on that campus, pray for the students and faculty, and just hang out with those who come.

8. Tour the Facility

This may not be the first thing to come to mind in getting to know a campus, but it can be very beneficial. Call the school's facilities department (look for the number online or just ask when calling the main line). Let them know you're from a church and would like a tour of some of their facilities for future potential events. I'd recommend asking to see the theater, lecture halls, or gymnasium. This tour does a few different things. First, it gets you on campus and even into areas you wouldn't likely see otherwise. Second, you get approximately a half hour with a staff member. During the tour ask some basic questions about the students, culture of the school, and even about the values of the faculty. Third, you open the door for an ongoing relationship with this staff member. This may or may not happen; but if you click, that person can be a great resource in the future. Let's just say facilities people have keys to everything. I'll leave it at that.

While these are effective ideas for commuter schools, your best connections with students on commuter campuses will be through your existing relationships with students who attend that school. So be patient, available, willing to invest in those students you do know, and prayerfully sit back and ask God to open doors for you.

NON-COMMUTER SCHOOLS

Doing church-based ministry in a context with a major university nearby can bring lots of wonderful opportunities, but it also brings some serious challenges. Unfortunately there is a huge florescent pink elephant in the room that everybody recognizes but few are addressing. And that's the frequent tension between church-based and campus-based ministry leaders. It's sad to say, but there's often a sense of competition between the two. Tension builds when everyone's out to build his own program, yet going after the same people. But it doesn't have to be this way. If we stay focused on discipleship and assimilation, there's no reason why our churches can't complement the work of campus ministries.

Both sides, church- and campus-ministry leaders, need to seriously reconsider how they approach the other. There should never be competition between ministries. We're on the same team, and we have to let every aspect of territorial arrogance and personal ego go. Instead of competing, we need to join forces. If there is a ministry on a campus, then as a church-based leader the last thing you should do is go into that campus and ignore what God is already doing there through that ministry. For instance rather than create a new wheel, the best way to put an end to any sense of competition is by

> If we stay focused on discipleship and assimilation, there's no reason why our churches can't complement the work of campus ministries.

serving *in* those campus ministries. Rather than duplicating efforts, it makes much more sense to join forces, come alongside each other, and support each other with our resources.

My friend Matt Metzger has done a great job with this. As a church-based college-ministry leader at Blackhawk Church in Madison, Wisconsin, he's figured some things out. He does some very simple things that have effectively helped him develop ongoing and healthy relationships with major campus ministries.

I recently talked with Matt about this and asked him what the most important element has been for him in bridging this gap. Here's what he said:

> The biggest thing is a lack of trust between church and campus leaders, so I've worked really hard to develop that by building relationships with them. My schedule is busy with so many things for our ministry, church, and my family; so my relationships with campus leaders will never be my top priority. But that doesn't mean I can't put some time and energy into them. I genuinely want to work together with the campus-ministry leaders as we seek to reach students on campus. I don't just want to play nicely in the sandbox, I want to be on the same team with them.

Matt was very clear about this. He genuinely seeks friendships with campus-ministry leaders. Granted, he's not going to be close to everyone, but there are a few people he's connected with. There's one guy he goes to the gym with every week, and he's gotten to know another one so well that their families vacation together. His relationship with these leaders has built the trust in ministry. It isn't a competition. As his great word picture says it, they're not just playing nicely in the sandbox—they are genuinely working together.

It's very important to remember that these relationships cannot be built overnight. Matt has been at this church for 10 years. By doing some very simple things, one at a time over the years, he's been able to develop trust with the campus leaders. You may work full time in a vocation and not have time during the day to spend with campus leaders like Matt does.[33] But regardless of your situation, there are some things you can do to be

---

33. I have a ton of respect for Matt. He's been faithful in one place for a long time and loves the students he works with. He's focused on relationships, and I think he's a great example for anyone working in college ministry.

intentional about these relationships. Here are some things Matt has found to be effective in his own life and ministry:

1. *Serve them in everyday life.* Look for practical ways you can serve campus-ministry leaders. Does someone need help on a house project? Go help. Not to promote your ministry, but on the basis of your friendship.

2. *Promote their events.* Instead of duplicating events, work with the campus leaders on theirs. There will, of course, be times when you do things for your ministry, but also push students to attend their events.

3. *Invite them to your house for dinner.* Make connections through community or campus events like a prayer breakfast. Then as you get to know people better, invite them and their families over for dinner.

4. *Travel together to conferences.* When a ministry conference comes up, look for opportunities to travel together and even room with others from your area.

5. *Pray together.* Take part in or organize times to join with other leaders in the area to pray for the campuses and ministries.

6. *Plan events together.* Whether it's a worship night or outreach event, plan it together. One of the most positive outcomes of doing this is that the students see the ministry leaders working together. This alone breaks down walls, allows relationships to build, and creates unity among believers.

MORE IDEAS FOR UNITY

To end this chapter I want to give you a few more practical things you can do as a church-based leader to help build a trusting relationship with campus leaders.

1. Search Your Own Heart

Work through any bitterness or competition you've been feeling. You don't have to agree with everything a particular ministry does; but at the very least, you must be the person who seeks unity with campus ministries. If you can't get past personal competitiveness, bitterness, or judgment, you don't need to read any further or try to bridge the gap. You won't get anywhere if you start with mixed motivations.

2. Meet Regularly with the Campus-Ministry Leader

Have coffee or lunch together once every couple of months so you can build a genuine relationship. Ask that leader how you can pray for the ministry. Offer your support and ask nothing in return. Most of all, mean it.

3. Offer Your Church Facilities

Let them know they're welcome to use your church spaces—free of charge—for anything they need or want to do. Providing services to them breaks down any walls they may have built up on their side. Yes, this suggestion also exposes college-age people to what's going on in your church, but that exposure can't be your motivation. This invitation is about serving the campus ministry, not building yours.

4. If Possible, Offer to Help a Ministry Financially

You may want to designate a portion of your own budget (if you have one!) toward a campus ministry. Personal fundraising alone supports most of these ministries, so a little financial help to sponsor an event is always appreciated. If they're holding a car wash or other fundraiser, go help them. These small gestures go a long way toward building trust and unity.

5. Seek the Leader's Advice for Your Ministry

Chances are they have great insights into life on campus and the struggles college students are facing. They've likely developed a great ministry philosophy that meets these needs. There's no reason to compete when it comes to serving college-age people. They need all the care and guidance they can get.

6. Join Forces on Outreach Events

Come alongside another ministry, serving them in any way you can. Whether it's helping put up posters, handing out flyers, being a part of planning meetings, loaning them a portable sound system, or simply letting them use the church photocopy machine, extra hands and minds are always welcome.

7. Connect Older People in Your Church with the Campus Ministry

Showing students the benefits of having older believers in their lives can help them connect to a local church. Even if they don't connect to your church, hopefully you will have provided an experience that will make them feel more comfortable wherever they do connect. Your role can be exposing them to the church body and to life beyond their campus. In my mind, that's a phenomenal ministry!

8. Consider Mentoring a Campus-Ministry Leader

Many of these ministries have staff members who are right out of college themselves and who might appreciate learning from your experience. Once you've established a trusting relationship with the ministry leader, ask your friend if a mentoring relationship would be helpful. And if it would be, make it happen.

THE BOTTOM LINE

- The best place to begin reaching a campus is with the people already in your ministry.

- Take the time to get to know the unique culture of the school you wish to reach.

- Campus ministry is not a competition—be intentional about forming lasting relationships with the people already working on campus.

NOTES:

CHAPTER 18

WHEN STUDENTS ARE AWAY AT SCHOOL

Raul is a pastor in a small town outside Milwaukee, Wisconsin.[34] It's a rural farming community where everyone tends to know everyone. There's an elementary school and a junior high that's connected to a high school totaling about 200 kids. His church has about 150 people, including kids, which is fairly large for this area. The tough part of his ministry context is that once kids graduate from high school, they move away for college. He desperately wants to continue his ministry to these kids, but he's perplexed about how to do that effectively.

Leaders in churches like this one have an internal struggle that leaves many with more unanswered questions than answered. Youth pastors across the country see their kids take off, and they don't know whether they should stay connected, let them go, or what. They love these kids, and they want to see them continue to grow and stay connected to their church in some way. But figuring out what that looks like can be a bit difficult—especially if they're processing it in a vacuum.

Continuing ministry to young adults who go away to school can be challenging. And finding a balance between keeping in touch and allowing kids to separate in healthy ways can be a challenge, too. Whether college-age people move one hour away or across the country to attend school, keeping in touch with them takes a great deal of intentionality on our part.

> Staying connected to college students who move away is not difficult but takes a great deal of intentionality.

But it's not difficult. There are some simple things we can do. We just have to be intentional. Even though I haven't worked in rural towns like Raul's, I've still had students move away to school, and I often talk with others in similar situations. We all share the common desire to stay connected to

---

34. His name has been changed to protect his privacy.

those students—at least to some degree. We want to let them know that our church still loves them and they have a church family to come back to if they so choose.

The following are 10 strategies to adopt or adapt for your own situation in ministering to students who leave.

10 WAYS TO CONTINUE MINISTRY

1. Send Them Off Well

Too many youth pastors and church leaders tend to forget about people who are leaving . . . even before they leave. But I've found that sending them off well is a crucial element to staying connected to them after they leave. You can do a lot of different things, such as making a campus visit with your high school students as a scouting trip or even moving them to college. Either way it shows them you're not dropping them. Instead, you're excited about their next stage of life, want to be a part of it, and will be there to support them. Trust me, this involvement from the beginning will keep the door open for a relationship while they're away. It could even be worth assigning part of your budget (if you have one) to the cost of traveling. While you're on campus, meet with some local pastors to find out what kind of support they offer college students. Then let your student know what options are available for church participation.

2. Do Some Homework

Prior to their leaving do some basic searches on the Internet for churches in the area. Send some emails to college-ministry pastors (or youth pastors or pastors) at churches close to the school. Talk to them about their philosophy of ministry, doctrine, how they see incoming freshmen fitting into their church, and so on. Building this type of relationship lays the groundwork—and is very much appreciated by both college students and their parents. After getting to know the pastor and possibly listening to some podcasts, you may be able to recommend a church. Then follow up to see how things are going and whether or not a connection is happening. Having you walk alongside them in this process will mean more to them than you realize. The student may or may not get involved there, but the effort is still worth making.

3. Pick Up the Phone

We don't realize how much a random phone call can mean to someone. While you're driving around and a student pops into your mind, don't just think about that person—call! If the student doesn't pick up, leave a message saying you were just thinking about him or her. I usually add that I wasn't calling for any particular reason and the student doesn't have to call me back. If the student does pick up, I ask if it's a good time to talk. If so, then I ask how life is going, what the student is up to, and how I can pray for him or her. I've found that simply picking up the phone every once in a while makes a huge difference.

4. Develop a Facebook Group Strictly for Graduates from Your Church

Make this group invite-only. This way you can post blog updates, send messages, and keep up with what's going on in the lives of your graduates. This social-networking group can also be a way for your students to stay in contact with each other. You can even use this group to set up random chat meetings or gatherings you'll be putting together over the holidays.

5. Pay Attention to Important Times in Their School Year—Particularly Finals Week

Make sure you call your students during this time to let them know you're praying for them. If you can, send care packages with movie coupons or gift certificates to a local coffee shop. It's a small gesture that will mean a lot.

6. Send Care Packages from the Whole Church

It's one thing for *you* to mail a package, but it's something else for students to get a care package from their church family. Sending rolls of quarters for laundry machines, laundry soap, or gift certificates to fast-food restaurants can go a long way toward making sure these students know they haven't been forgotten. Again, there might not be a ton of ongoing conversation with the student; but believe me, having a home base at this point in their lives can mean the world to them.

7. Host a Blog for Graduates

You can write posts on what you've been thinking about, recap the messages from your church services, update them on what's happening back home, or have a few students rotate the blogging responsibilities. One of the most effective blog elements we've come up with is to have older believers from the church post messages from time to time. They write about the ways they've been praying for our college students and might even share a few stories about their own college days. Regardless of how you use the blog, it's a great interactive point of connection.

8. Point Them to Ministries Like Liveabove.com

This ministry deals with more than 4,000 campuses and more than 1,000 military bases. They've compiled a database of high school grads from all over the world who are attending a college and want to connect with a local church. College ministries (or churches in general) can register as well and get the contact information of freshmen coming to their area. Once your students find a church, do a little homework so you know what kind of church it is. If you have concerns, share them; but I've found this site to be a great tool for students who want to find a church while they're away at college.

9. Help Them Get Involved with a Campus Ministry

Christian campus groups are a good way to make sure students have an immediate avenue for connecting with others. If they don't connect soon after they arrive at school, they may never do so. Call the person who heads up the ministry and make a point to let that person know you've got students coming to the school. Let your students know you care enough about them to make sure they get involved. If you can, get the ministry leader and your students connected through email, phone, an online network, or in person when you go with them on a campus visit (hint!).

10. Text or Email Often and Randomly

Better yet, ask other people to do the same. Overloading students with messages from a bunch of people trying to keep in touch can be a turn-off. But encouraging their small group leader and possibly another adult in the church to randomly check in on them can be very encouraging. Sometimes it can be timely as well. Students have often told me that these text messages or emails came at just the right time. I've had many tell me that the day the message arrived was a tough one, or how the short text that said I JUST PRAYED FOR YOU encouraged them.

It's important to remember that most of this stuff doesn't take a lot of our time, but it does go a long way in our relationships with students. Nearly every college student deals with a sense of loneliness and detachment. Your occasional call, text, or package—not to mention your efforts to help them get connected with ministries on campus—will let them know they're not alone and there's someone out there who loves them. With simple things like this, you can be one of the most encouraging people in a college student's life.

HOME FOR THE HOLIDAYS

College students are known to pop in on their parents, do their laundry, visit for a little while, and then leave with grocery bags filled with food. But those are the students who go to school fairly close to home. Others who move farther away find themselves coming home only for Thanksgiving and Christmas, potentially over spring break, and then again (at least for a little while) during the summer—that is, if they don't have a job close to school. Their times at home are few and far between, but they're important nevertheless.

Regardless of how far away they attend school, most students have a sense of excitement about coming home for a time. But it's important to note that it's a temporary excitement. They've begun their own lives, and even though it can be tough at times, most like the separation they now have. The college-age years are a time of independent exploration away from what they grew up with. Visits back home can be great times to connect with students, but they can also be a bit awkward.

The biggest thing to keep in mind is the awkwardness students may feel in some of their relationships—particularly in dating relationships. Some kept their dating relationship with their high school sweetheart going, even though it was long distance. They may be excited to see each other, but it doesn't mean the relationship isn't a bit awkward. A lot has happened in their lives apart from each other that's, well, simply impossible to share.

And as much as iChat or Skype can help, the lives of the two individuals have been light years apart.

This relational awkwardness doesn't stop with dating, either. It's often noticeable with best friends, parents, and maybe even you. The fact is that their lives at school are packed with new experiences, new friends, new feelings, confusion, and clarity. To try to articulate everything in one visit is daunting, to say the least. As honest as they might want to be about their time away, to fully disclose what they've done, felt, or gone through is impossible. Many come home and don't know what to say. Some have compromised their faith and feel a sense of guilt and shame when they're home. Some will put up a façade, some will be standoffish, while others will come in repentance.

> The college-age years are a time of independent exploration away from what they grew up with. Returning home can be exciting but often awkward.

Yet on the other side of the fence are those who are very excited to see you and others around church. But there is still too much to tell. And even though some are excited, they're not likely to disclose everything, and they might possibly miss some of the most significant things during their time away. But that's okay. We don't need to know everything.

Having said that, we can try to find out how they're really doing, what their lives are really like, and if they're discouraged about things or excited about others. So it's important to keep some boundaries and balance in your conversations. Here are four recommendations for hanging out with students while they're home on break:

1. Ask Direct or Specific Questions

Asking an open-ended question like, "So how was your semester?" can be overwhelming and actually lead them to feel as though they can't connect with you. To think through and articulate everything in that short amount of time is too much, and your students can leave feeling as though their lives are too separate from yours. I've found it's much better to ask specifically about their roommates, favorite classes, closest friends at school, involvement in campus ministry (or lack of), favorite or most frustrating classes, or even if it's a bit awkward for them to come home...things like that.

2. Share About Your Personal Life

Pursuing your students for a time of coffee or lunch is good. But from their perspective, it can come across as being formal—maybe even resembling an accountability time or interview. This can be okay, but I've found it's *much* better if you take off the pastor hat and share about yourself. Now is the time to intentionally begin treating them like friends—especially if they were in your high school ministry. This can really bridge any separation and kill any awkwardness they may be feeling about their home church. Talking to them as a peer can make a world of difference in reconnecting with them. Sharing about your own struggles, doubts, family life, and so on can be a great next step for your relationship—that is, as long as you don't dominate the conversation!

3. Ask for Prayer Requests

At the end of your conversation, specifically ask them for *one* thing you can pray about. This lets them know they don't leave your mind when they return to school and your relationship with them means more to you than just being a part of the job! Periodically over the next few months, make sure you send them a text message (or six) letting them know you're still praying for that specific thing.

4. Ask Them if They're Encouraged

You could get a whole spectrum of answers from this one, but it's a great question to ask. Some might break into tears, while others will simply be encouraged that you asked. Either way, I've found it to be a great question. It can also give you insight into areas where you can personally encourage them. Some will be more open about this than others, but you may want to ask them specifically about their relationships with their parents, an ex, or their best friend from high school; if they have a sense of direction in life; and so on.

LAST (QUICK) THOUGHT

The key to continuing a ministry to college-age people while they're away at school is staying in contact and letting them know you're thinking about them. If you can accomplish those two things, your ministry continues.

THE BOTTOM LINE

- Our job isn't finished when students move away to attend school.

- To have a ministry to college students who are away at school is simple and doesn't have to take a lot of time. But it's vital.

- More than nurturing a relationship with us as individuals, we want to encourage an ongoing connection with our churches.

NOTES:

Share Your Thoughts

With the Author: Your comments will be forwarded to
the author when you send them to *zauthor@zondervan.com*.

With Zondervan: Submit your review of this book
by writing to *zreview@zondervan.com*.

Free Online Resources at
www.zondervan.com

Zondervan AuthorTracker: Be notified whenever your favorite
authors publish new books, go on tour, or post an update
about what's happening in their lives at www.zondervan.com/
authortracker.

Daily Bible Verses and Devotions: Enrich your life with daily
Bible verses or devotions that help you start every morning
focused on God. Visit www.zondervan.com/newsletters.

Free Email Publications: Sign up for newsletters on Christian
living, academic resources, church ministry, fiction, children's
resources, and more. Visit www.zondervan.com/newsletters.

Zondervan Bible Search: Find and compare Bible passages in
a variety of translations at www.zondervanbiblesearch.com.

Other Benefits: Register yourself to receive online benefits
like coupons and special offers, or to participate in research.

ZONDERVAN.com/
AUTHORTRACKER
follow your favorite authors